"Pat" Patterson

For I dipt into the future,
        far as human eye could see,
Saw the Vision of the world,
        and all the wonder that would be;

Saw the heavens fill with commerce,
        argosies of magic sails,
Pilots of the purple twilight,
        dropping down with costly bales;

FROM THE POEM LOCKSLEY HALL
BY ALFRED LORD TENNYSON, 1842

"Pat" Patterson

by Frank J. Taylor

Illustrations by Gordon Brusstar

Lane Magazine & Book Company
Menlo Park, California

Foreword

This small volume makes no pretense of being a biography of William A. "Pat" Patterson, the extraordinary human dynamo who guided United Air Lines from its precarious birth to its prestigious status as the country's largest airline when he retired in 1966. Rather, it is a profile of his personality and a gathering of episodes and anecdotes emphasizing his unique business philosophy and his personal-touch way of running a great airline. To do a book was the inspiration of a group of the company's directors. They felt that the Patterson blueprint should be preserved for younger and future generations of the burgeoning United family. "Pat" Patterson didn't think a book was necessary to perpetuate his ideas or point up his achievements. He has always felt that United's people would be monument enough. "If you have the right people behind you, you're bound to look good," is his creed. But he consented to talk about how he found these right people out along the airline, how their ideas rubbed off on him, and how he rubbed them off on others. All his life he has been a veritable incubator of ideas and a do-it-now implementer of them. In this book I have tried to capture the spirit and the personality of this unique airways empire builder. Part of this effort is in text about him; some more of it is in brief and pithy quotations from his talks and from interviews with him. I make no claim to being objective and offer no apology for being biased. Like everyone else I know who has felt the Patterson touch for the past three decades, I am an unabashed Patterson buff.

FRANK J. TAYLOR

Contents

CHAPTER I

Genesis of a Flying-Machine Man

It was one of those fortuitous happenstances that changed the flight plan of history. The happenstance, on this March day in 1927, was that all of the other executives of prestigious Wells Fargo-Nevada Bank in San Francisco were out for lunch. To tend the bank they had left the man on the lowest officer rung, a natty and diminutive go-getter, 27-year-old newly appointed assistant vice president William Allan Patterson. Sitting at a front desk and alert for a new account, Patterson spotted a hesitant, genteel stranger looking about furtively. Bouncing over to greet the visitor, he asked, "Can we do anything for you, sir?"

"I thought so when I came in," replied the caller, "but I guess not."

"Have a seat. Let's talk about it," urged Patterson.

The diffident prospective customer introduced himself as Vern C. Gorst, founder and president of Pacific Air Transport, an airline he had launched on a frayed shoestring to carry the airmail between Los Angeles, San Francisco, Portland, and Seattle on a Post Office contract. PAT flew what was then one of the country's most hazardous airways.

The over-optimistic promoter had swapped shares in his company for planes, gasoline, pilots' services, and for dollars whenever he could get them. Between paychecks from the U. S. Post Office, his treasury was bare. What he desperately needed at the moment, Gorst explained, was a $5,000 loan. He proposed to use some of the money to raise an ill-fated plane out of San Francisco Bay to salvage an engine, which he could buy cheap.

Under Patterson's adroit questioning, Gorst concluded that the salt water may have damaged the submerged engine beyond repair. Even so, the financial plight of the struggling airline intrigued the young banker. Eager to bag his first new account, he visited PAT's hangars at Crissy Field that very afternoon. After checking Gorst's airmail contract, chatting with pilots and looking over equipment, he wound up the day by making his first loan. It was for $5,000, exactly what Gorst had come in to borrow, to tide the airline over until the next Post Office paycheck came in.

The following morning an apprehensive junior officer found himself on the carpet in the office of Wells Fargo's austere president, Frederick L. Lipman.

"About that loan you made to the flying machine company," began Lipman sternly. "I don't think the flying machine business is a very good risk."

The bank's new business-getter stood his ground, making a stout defense of the idea that one good way to build new accounts would be to help struggling small companies become airborne, Pacific Air Transport in particular. His cautious chief was unconvinced.

"I'm not worried about losing the bank's money, Willie," he assured Patterson. "But if your first loan goes sour it might undermine your confidence. Stick by those flying machine men until they pay back."

That did it. The skeptical president's instructions lost the bank an up-and-coming young officer and gained for the fledgling air transport industry a spirited and daring pacemaker. Aviation was in the air in the spring of 1927. In San Diego an ex-airmail pilot known as "Slim" Lindbergh was readying a Ryan monoplane for the first electrifying solo flight from New York to Paris; Lindbergh had chosen the Ryan partly because of its performance for Vern Gorst's flying postmen. Across San Francisco Bay, Army Signal Corps fliers Hegenberger and Maitland were tuning another flying machine to conquer the Pacific's watery stretches by winging from Oakland to Honolulu. Fascinated by the conquests of the skies, Patterson did stick by the flying machine men. He spent most of his spare time with them, becoming more enchanted each day by their challenging venture.

Once, in his late teens, he had squandered two weeks' earnings on a 20-minute ride in a flying crate with cracks in the floor boards through which he had a scary view of San Francisco Bay. Another time, just as his name was called for a flight, another sky-rider cracked up. He was watching Lincoln Beachy stunt for exposition crowds when a wing came off and the daredevil crashed to his death. Despite these hair-raising experiences, Patterson was a flying enthusiast. The intrepid pilots were his heroes. Now they were pioneering a brave young industry with their frail flying machines. The prospects were contagious.

The flying machine men repaid the $5,000 loan promptly. Patterson still stuck with them. When Gorst received a $15,000 check from the Post Office for flying the mail, Patterson talked him into investing the money in U.S. government bonds. With these as collateral, even Wells Fargo's top echelon approved a new loan to Pacific Air Transport. The financial sleight-of-hand established the credit of the flying machine men.

Vern Gorst was still strapped for funds to pay for planes, gasoline, and meet his payroll. Patterson spent his off-duty hours trying to relieve the acute financial pains of the flying machine men. He set up an orderly system of accounting. Gorst had a bin of used spare parts which he called his depreciation reserve; Patterson established a bookkeeping depreciation account. Once when Gorst was unable to meet a payroll, Patterson put up as collateral for a loan several thousand dollars in Liberty Bonds that he had just inherited from his grandfather. Another time, while riding a PAT airmail plane north, he was stranded with several pilots by foul weather one weekend in Medford, Oregon. They groused that Gorst was paying their wages in PAT stock, which bought no groceries.

"We'll get some money for you," promised Patterson. Back in San Francisco, he braced officials of the Standard Oil Company, which advanced a credit of $25,000, part of it cash, that pulled the airline through another emergency. It was the best credit Standard ever advanced; four decades later, selling fuel to the flying machine men had grown into Standard's largest commercial account. But in 1927, the advance was a wild gamble and the only security was the forthright integrity and faith of the imaginative young banker who, without realizing it, had become a flying machine man himself at heart.

Four decades later, at age 65, short and stocky and still bouncy "Pat" Patterson emerged on another spring morning in 1965 from a board meeting in New York's Waldorf-Astoria Hotel. With the same boyish gleam in his dark brown eyes, he told waiting reporters how he had just placed a record order for jetliners, $750 million worth of speedy sky transports for United Air Lines, the world's largest airline that had burgeoned out of the shaky flying machine business to which he had made his first $5,000 loan. He had stretched the credit established back in 1927 for the flying machine men, to borrow thousands of times $5,000 to pay for the additional jetliners for United's fleet. Over the four decades, Patterson had invested close to $3 billion in flying machines and facilities to keep them flying. That new business account he had brought in for doubtful Mr. Lipman now carried a routine $2 million balance at Wells Fargo.

In April of 1966, on the 40th anniversary of United Air Lines' humble beginnings, Patterson retired from the flying machine business, after flying as many millions of miles as many of his veteran pilots. Mr. Lipman's concern about his ability to make sound deci-

Our Greatest Resource: The Individual

INDIVIDUALISM THRIVES *best in an atmosphere of freedom, such as we have in this country. There are controls, but our system of competitive enterprise offers ample latitude for achievement. You who inherit this system are its trustees. It will be in your custody to improve or impair. It's a wonderfully productive mechanism and it provides the world's highest standard of living. Granted there are imperfections but they are small in relation to total benefits. We must not be blind to social problems—to grievous defects in housing, health and education. Each of us has an obligation to take part in good works. The man who follows his own narrow way, heedless of misfortune around him, supplies government with reasons to go beyond its proper area. That area was defined many years ago by a man of great compassion, Abraham Lincoln. He said that government's proper role is to do for people what needs to be done that they cannot of themselves do at all or do so well.*

W.A.P.

sions proved unfounded. He could still make them. Many of these decisions were not only milestones in his life but in the air transport business as well.

The innovations he had pioneered were sometimes rated at first as expensive and nonessential foolishment by the practical fliers who launched several rival lines. Most of these "Patterson follies" have since been adopted as sound, commonplace airline practices. Among them were: the first stewardesses, thereby launching a new global profession for women; the first reliable ground-plane communications; guaranteed pay for pilots whether they flew or not; mechanical flight analyzers to double-check pilots' skill; the first four-engine airliner; the pioneer weather radar-equipped fleet; economy coach travel; the country's first domestic jetliner fleet; flight kitchens to provide in-flight meals; the first airline retirement program; a university of the air to make sure that though "our airplanes may become obsolete, our people never will."

These are only a few typical Patterson innovations. On his retirement a competitor admitted grudgingly, "There's only one Pat Patterson and they lost the mold." To those who know him, this is understandable. All his life, Patterson has thrived on change. He has picked other people's minds for their brainstorms, which he delighted in putting into practice. Most empire builders, when they get their empires molded, want to keep them that way. Patterson hasn't. He has liked his empire of the air in a state of flux. He has doted on imagineering what air transport will be like a decade or a quarter century hence. His staff economists have always worked like beavers with charts and computers projecting the future. Sometimes Patterson has bought these futures, sometimes he hasn't. After several bouts with a business ailment he calls "analysis paralysis," he is wary of it. His antidote has always been a good stiff shot of common sense.

The key turning point in his life, Pat Patterson says, was the evening of his first day at Wells Fargo Bank, where he landed a job late in 1914 as a $25-a-month messenger boy. As he was checking out at the end of his first day's work, he was hailed by assistant cashier F. I. Raymond.

"Where are you going, son?" asked Raymond.

"To get some supper, then home."

"Come over here and sit down. Let's talk a bit. Then you have supper with me," said Raymond, a tall, outgiving former Australian. While Raymond slowly rolled a cigaret, he asked why young Patterson wasn't going on to high school.

"I have to help support my mother," explained the youngster.

"If you want to get ahead, you'll have to keep on studying," said Raymond. "People will never criticize you for not having an education, but they will if you don't try to get one."

The banker took his new friend across the street to a cafeteria for an early supper. Then they boarded a street car to Humboldt High School, which Raymond had attended at night for several years to educate himself. Raymond helped the new office boy enroll in evening courses that might help him get ahead at Wells Fargo. This night school study stretched out to 13 years during which the diligent student finished his high school training and completed almost three years of college courses. Raymond was always on hand to help choose new courses of study, or to pull his hard working young protégé out of a class when he felt that Patterson had soaked up enough of what it had to offer. During one summer vacation, Raymond gave his young friend a handful of letters of introduction to bankers in other cities and a railroad ticket and sent him around the country, the one and only time he put up money. Raymond believed in helping people help themselves, a gospel that became a fundamental in Patterson's book.

"If I had walked into the arms of a union organizer after that first day at Wells Fargo, instead of into F. I. Raymond, I might have sought security as an office boy," Patterson says half in jest. "Instead I had all the advantage of complete insecurity."

Other Wells Fargo officers took the bright, energetic messenger under their wing, and left a deep impression on his life. One in particular was Frank B. King, who interested himself in Patterson's personal welfare. On one occasion when a flu epidemic laid both Patterson and his mother low, King dispatched a doctor to their home to make sure they had adequate medical care. Another was Arthur D. Oliver, who hired him.

For the neat, small, energetic and impressionable youth, these character-forming years in San Francisco filled a gap — the lack of a normal family life during his boyhood.

By 1916, the Wells Fargo executives had picked him for a comer and had launched him on a round of duties that gave him unusual banking experience for a youngster. On the day he was promoted to a teller's cage, his reputation was established; he spotted a forged check — "a clever piece of work by Willie Patterson," to quote the records of the bank's office administration committee. In 1920, in a confidential personnel report, the committee rated young Patterson "Number 1" in attendance, on-time arrival, courtesy, initiative, enthusiasm, aptitude, output of work, loyalty, trustworthiness, self-confidence, and personality. But only "Number 2" in co-operation and executive ability. The records also reveal a forthright "beef" written in Willie Patterson's then fine script:

"Gentlemen: I have been reporting to the Transit Dept. (the mail room) for nearly five years. Such men as Stone, Lee, Gilstrap,

Sewell and a few others have not reported for a good many weeks, in fact, some have never reported. I claim seniority over all these men and have also put in some long hours in this bank and therefore I should also be excused."

The "beef" got results. Within two weeks another man was reporting early to sort the incoming mail. Willie Patterson was enjoying bankers' hours.

A turning point in Patterson's youth was the evening when he was taken home by Ned Stone, a young colleague at the bank. Home was a big house on Chestnut Street which Stone shared with 15 other live wires, all college graduates on the make in brokerage, banking, insurance, shipping, merchandising, and advertising careers. A Mrs. Clark and her daughter ran the place for them. It was like a small college fraternity in the heart of the city. When they were not gathered around the piano, the roommates were trying out brainstorms on each other, or arguing in bull sessions. When Patterson's widowed mother remarried, he was invited to move into the big house. His fellow boarders quickly changed his nickname from "Willie" to "Pat." He has been "Pat" Patterson ever since.

For Patterson, rounding out his studies at University of California evening classes, these years were a near approach to college campus life. He soaked up like a sponge the social amenities that his more fortunate roommates had absorbed on "the Stanford Farm." Ideas sprouted like beanstalks in the big house. This simulated fraternity life polished his gregarious, easy-mixing manner and whetted his insatiable curiosity. During the five years that he lived with the group, he blossomed into a self-confident, easily-approached extrovert who could find a common ground for discussion with anybody about anything on the other fellow's terms. It was a schooling that stood him well in later years.

For the eager embryo banker, these happy character-forming San Francisco days were a far cry from his lost boyhood on the rolling Waipahu sugar plantation near Honolulu's Pearl Harbor. He was born in a Honolulu hospital on October 1, 1899. His childhood home was the picturesque Waipahu sugar company town, where his Scotch-Irish father, also a William A. Patterson, was "head luna" or boss of the plantation's several thousand Japanese workers. His grandfather was "water luna," in charge of irrigation of the cane fields. On some days, strenuous head luna Patterson wore out three horses riding the gummy cane fields stretching over rugged plateaus and valleys. These were troubled times at Waipahu. The Japanese workers were angrily striking for more pay and better working conditions. Patterson's earliest recollection of his father is seeing him ride, crackling blacksnake whip in hand, into angry crowds of shouting, rock-throwing strikers. When the workers finally won, one of the conditions of the settlement was that "head luna Patterson must go." The company sent him to Puerto Rico to launch a new sugar plantation. His wife and son stayed on at Waipahu with the grandfather. The boy picked up Japanese words from his nurse before he learned to speak English from his mother and grandfather.

Like many other Islanders, Patterson was a mixture of nationalities. His mother, Mary Castro Patterson, was a descendant of early, devout Catholic Portuguese immigrants who came from the Azores to Hawaii when it was an independent kingdom. Thus he was like the Island preacher who lamented, "The Hawaiian and Chinese in me are always fighting." In Patterson's case, the Scotch and Portuguese genes seldom fought, but all his life his impulses have begun with a warm Latin emotional approach which prevailed up to the point where his hard-headed Scotch judgment asserted itself. These useful Scotch genes must have been inherited. He saw but little of his father, who contracted "Panama fever," as malaria was known then, in Puerto Rico. He managed to get back to San Francisco where his wife and son joined him. He died when "Billy" Patterson was seven years old.

The father's death was a staggering upheaval for Mary Patterson and her small son. At the urging of the boy's grandfather, she returned to Hawaii. A tiny, sedate woman educated in Catholic convents, she attempted to adjust to an unsheltered life, without servants, carriages, the amenities of a plantation manager's home. When William Patterson lay on his deathbed, a priest had refused

An Airline Is People

THAT BIG JETLINER *in front of the airport is no better than the mind that flies it and the minds on the ground that service it and guide it. An airline is people as well as routes and planes. Everybody working for United should be moving ahead or knowing the reason why. Every employee should be evaluated frequently. It is his supervisor's responsibility to tell him honestly whether he is going ahead or standing still or slipping backward. After the supervisor has gone over the evaluation sheet with an employee, the latter signs it, making a note if he doesn't agree. This goes into his record and he knows he can talk it over later with the supervisor.*

This system started two decades back when I told the head of Personnel, "See all those young people. They must have ambitions we don't know about. Let's ask them what they want to be in United." So we interviewed several hundred of them individually. About 65 percent wanted to be let alone. Fifteen percent had ideas of grandeur but were doing little to improve themselves. Twenty percent knew where they wanted to go, what their qualifications were, and what they had to do to rise. Now, 20 percent of 37,000 employees gives you a great reservoir of talent. It is the company's obligation, and a good investment as well, to set up a system for finding that 20 percent.

W.A.P.

19

him last rites because he was a Protestant. A Methodist minister comforted her in her bereavement. She renounced her faith, taking her small son with her into the Methodist church and later became a Christian Scientist. This experience germinated an exceptional tolerance in Pat Patterson.

Breadwinning was difficult in Hawaii. After six years Mary Patterson gave up the struggle and sailed for San Francisco, where she had relatives, to go to a business school. With financial help from grandfather Patterson, she enrolled her son in a military academy near Diamond Head. The school was run by a strict martinet headmaster and the boy hated it. After three weeks he ran away. Caught and hauled back, he was deprived of his privileges and shorn of his hoarded pocket money. He promptly made another escape, this time keeping under cover as he made his way to the Waikiki end of the car line. A big-hearted Hawaiian woman gave him food and carfare to downtown Honolulu. At the waterfront he found an old four-masted schooner about to sail for San Francisco. The diminutive 13-year-old talked the skipper into signing him on as cabin boy.

The voyage to California on the sugar schooner *Annie Johnson* turned out to be a 23-day nightmare. The ship was no sooner beyond the reef than her cabin boy turned a seasick green, partly from the rolling seas, more from the sickly sweet odor of raw sugar wafting out of the hold. The first night out he tried to keep on his feet in the cook's galley. After that, he lay in his bunk, too weak to stand for most of the rough passage. When the *Annie Johnson* finally docked at San Francisco Bay, he vowed never again to put to sea. The memory of the awful voyage haunted Patterson for half of his life. He clung to his vow until May 1, 1947, when United Air Lines launched its plushy DC-6 service on the San Francisco-Honolulu route. For this gala occasion the United staff induced him to fly to Hawaii, eight smooth overseas hours on the Mainliner *Hawaii*. The flight partially erased the vow; Patterson still refuses to cross oceans on surface ships, though he has winged to Hawaii repeatedly and to Europe. His homecoming to Hawaii, at age 47, was the gala return of a famous son. The happy Islanders stacked leis around Patterson's neck until he needed a periscope to see the hula girls gyrating in his honor. Patterson forgot the horrors of his *Annie Johnson* voyage and, in later years, was able to gaze without becoming queasy in the solar plexus at an authentic scale model of the old schooner, a gift from his admiring staff, enclosed in a plastic bubble on the wall in front of his desk.

After a reunion with his mother, who had found an apartment on Hayes Street, 13-year-old Billy Patterson enrolled in San Francisco's John Swett Grammar School. In his after-class and weekend hours he pioneered in various San Francisco industries not customarily associated with his name. In later years he was either "the former banker" or "the flying machine man." But his first enterprise was wrapping meat in a lower Market Street market Friday afternoons and Saturday for $2 a week. He soon changed from meats to other foods at Donavan's Grocery at Hayes and Laguna. Here his specialty was picking up butter and eggs and hot bread with a small wagon, for which he was both the driver and the horse. His small stature made him a poor substitute for a horse and he switched to an afternoon newspaper route. Here the Tom Sawyer in young Patterson came to the fore; he delivered papers to several saloons which set out free baked beans and pigs knuckles for patrons and he was able to farm out part of his newspaper delivering to other boys who had a taste for these delicacies. He forsook the newspaper business to sell programs after school at the baseball stadium. This enabled him to see the games free and get paid for it. The great "Buck" Weaver became his baseball hero. Weaver and several other players paid him a dollar per trip to tote their mitts, bats, and masks via ferry to Oakland where they played alternate games. The big payoff came after the games when he was allowed to keep the players' equipment overnight at home, where he could collect dimes from neighboring kids for the privilege of catching a few tosses with "Buck" Weaver's mitt or for making a few swings with his bat.

This lucrative bonanza came to an end when he graduated from John Swett Grammar School with a medal for exceptional scholarship. In the class graduating picture, it is easy to pick out

Billy Patterson, the neat little fellow in the back row with the high collar, tie, and carefully combed hair parted in the middle, a foretaste of the equally neat airline president of later years. After his commencement address at John Swett, forerunner of numerous pithy and philosophic public talks, Billy's mother said, "Now you must go on to high school." But the busy teen-age businessman had other ideas. He had spotted a help wanted ad for "Office boy — grammer school education, living with parents, age 16 to 17, no cigaret smoker, good opportunity for right boy, state salary expected, Box 3178 Examiner."

Though one year too young and living with only one parent, Patterson penned a bold-script letter to "Gentlemen: In answer to your ad in today's *Examiner,* wish to state that I am a boy 15 years of age, living at home with my mother, who is a widow. I am a recent graduate of the John Swett Grammar School. I am pleased to refer you to Miss A. H. Lahande, vice principal of John Swett School, also to the Latham Auto Supply Company [his mother's employer]. Hoping to receive an encouraging reply, I beg to remain, Very Truly Yours, William Patterson."

Patterson did receive an encouraging reply from "Box 3178 *Examiner*," who turned out to be Wells Fargo's assistant cashier Arthur D. Oliver. Invited to come down to the bank for an interview, Billy Patterson shrewdly stuck his scholarship medal in his pocket, along with letters of recommendation from his principal, his mother's employer, and a lawyer friend. None of the other applicants had medals. He got the job. This explains how he just happened to be heading for the door at the end of his first day at Wells Fargo when assistant cashier F. I. Raymond hailed him and directed him to the right fork of the road leading to Humboldt High night school. Raymond saw to it that Patterson's excellent marks in night school classes were duly recorded in the bank's office administration records. Others among the bank's officers kept an eye on him as he worked up to junior officer status at 27, when he was made assistant to Clare W. Banta, vice president in charge of new business. It was Banta who gave him authority to make his first loan to Vern Gorst. Actually Patterson didn't have the author-

It Takes
Time
to Grow
an Oak

Y OU HAVE AN IDEA? *Hang onto it! It's the most valuable thing in the world. Nurture it. Test it. And remember: you can grow a toadstool overnight but it takes time to grow an oak. I am engaged in what I believe to be the most thrilling industry in the world—aviation. My heart still leaps when I see a tiny two-seater plane soaring gracefully through the sky. Our great airliners awe me. Yet I know they were not produced in a day or a decade. It may take years to put your idea into action. But if it has real worth, time will prove it and you will have something that will endure.*

W.A.P.

ity to make that loan. He made it in Banta's name, and Banta stood behind it.

"When I look back at those early days, which were pretty tough, I feel sorry for the youngsters of today who miss those experiences," says Patterson. "You get something out of them. You learn to know what's going through the hearts and minds of people in trouble. I can live their troubles with them."

In 1923, while assiduously working up the Wells Fargo ramp, Patterson suddenly developed an obsession for the computing machines on the third floor of the head office building at Montgomery and Market Streets in San Francisco. At the slightest excuse he ran any mathematical problem through an office machine, even though it might be the simplest sort of adding or subtracting or multiplying. The inspiration for his newfound enthusiasm proved to be a University of California coed, Vera Anita Witt, who is remembered as the cutest adding machine operator Wells Fargo ever employed. The competition for Miss Witt's attention was not easy, even for resourceful Pat Patterson. Several other unmarried young Wells Fargo hopefuls had suddenly become office machine buffs, too.

Patterson has explained repeatedly since Vera Witt became his bride on June 20, 1924, that "I had to work like heck for her and I still do."

CHAPTER II

Birth of an Air Giant

Youthful banker Patterson has been called "the right man at the right time in the right place" to play the lead role in the drama of air transport in the United States. This is no exaggeration. But during the first years after his decisive loan to the flying machine men, he was merely the stand-in for the lead role. They were crucial years — in his life and the industry's. The hand of destiny seemed to be impelling him relentlessly into his lifetime flight path. The first hop in this flight was bringing order into the tangled web of Vern Gorst, promoter of Pacific Air Transport.

"All the experts of the day said an airplane would never be flown north of San Francisco because of the mountainous terrain," recalls Patterson. "Vern Gorst wasn't bothered by the mountains, but he surely was plagued by financial problems."

Gorst's part in pioneering air transportation is sometimes forgotten, but never by Patterson. Eager to be the first private enterpriser to carry the airmail on contract for the Post Office, Gorst had flown a hazardous pathfinding flight over the Siskiyous with Claude Ryan, San Diego designer and builder of the stout Ryan monoplane, the same sturdy craft that later carried Charles A. Lindbergh across the Atlantic. Gorst had ordered a fleet of Ryans, but he wasn't the first to fly them. When the monoplanes began rolling out of the Ryan plant, Gorst as usual was fresh out of cash to pay for them. Banker Patterson had not yet come into his life to find dollars for the impoverished airline. Gorst had to let Walter T. Varney, a San Francisco flying school operator, have the first four Ryans for his Pasco-Boise-Elko airmail route. Varney had already made history by flying a bag of mail over the Idaho-Nevada mountains on April 1, 1926, thus scooping Gorst as first airmail contractor to get off the ground. Like Gorst, Varney had found his original makeshift stunt planes too flimsy to fight through mountain passes. Unlike Gorst, he had the $8,700 Claude Ryan wanted for each monoplane. With the first four Ryans in service, Varney was able to extend his route to Seattle on the west and Salt Lake City on the east. It was a lucky buy; there came a day when the first air transport giant would bid a cool $2 million for the route.

Meantime, on September 15, 1926, promoter Gorst launched the Seattle-San Francisco-Los Angeles airmail service with planes of World War I vintage, some owned by the rash fliers who signed on as PAT pilots. A sensitive soul, Gorst was shaken to the marrow that first murderous winter as his pilots plunged into mountains or crashed in storms. It looked as though the Los Angeles aviation group headed by former racing driver Harris "Pop" Hanshue might be right. Hanshue had lost the Pacific Coast airmail contract mainly because he feared to bid on flights north of San Francisco. But after Vern Gorst got his Ryan monoplanes and his pilots had proved that flying the mail over the Siskiyous was feasible, the well-heeled Southern California aviation interests moved in with a plan to acquire PAT. Only the timely entry of banker Patterson on the scene saved the day.

The big postal plum in the west was the 1,918-mile San Francisco-Chicago route, which fed transcontinental airmail at Salt Lake City to short lines serving Los Angeles and the Pacific North-

Our People Are Our Capital

THE BALANCE SHEET *of United Air Lines places no dollars and cents value on our employees but in my opinion they represent the most important asset our company has on its books. In most businesses each morning on the desk of top management we find financial reports, sales reports, plant reports, capital investment and expenditures reports. But how many reports do we find on the desks of top management that deal with the vital statistics and the conditions of that great asset—employees? When I think of employees, including management people, I think of how we in business treat an expensive machine, the high value we place on it, the care with which we use and maintain it or shift it to another part of the plant, and the preparations we make before we retire it from service. That machine shows up in the balance sheet at the end of every month, along with other assets, and there is a dollar value attached to it which we know we want to preserve. It is unfortunate that there isn't something on that balance sheet to indicate the value of employees we work with every day. If we could just put down something about "20,000 employees, value $80 million," maybe we'd be considerably more conscious of their value.*

W.A.P.

west. The two big competitors for this bonanza contract were Western Air Express, the Southern California airline headed by Hanshue, and Boeing Air Transport, a subsidiary of Boeing Airplane Company, the Seattle builder of military planes. Early in 1927, Boeing captured the contract with a bid only two-thirds that of Western Air Express. It was so low that the Post Office made William E. Boeing, wealthy owner of Boeing Airplane Company, post an $800,000 bond to make sure that BAT would keep on flying the mail even at a loss. But instead of losing money, BAT turned in a profit from the first day of flight on July 1, 1927. BAT's secret of making money was a new type of mail plane, known as the Boeing 40, pulled hurriedly off the drawing boards by Boeing Airplane Company's versatile designer Claire L. Egtvedt. In the new model, the flying postmen still rode in open cockpits, but in front of the pilot was a tiny closed cabin in which two and later four passengers could squeeze tightly. The 40-A, as the early planes in this series were known, was powered by a revolutionary new air-cooled Wasp engine, originated by the Pratt & Whitney engine works at Hartford, Connecticut. With this development, water was not required in cooling the engine and such weight saving resulted in greater payload capacity.

These mail-passenger planes played an important role in Patterson's future. Still losing money, Vern Gorst thought his Pacific Air Transport could pull out of the red if he could buy some of the Boeing ships, which cost $25,000 apiece. This was exactly $25,000 more than Vern Gorst had to plank down. He was at a turning point and knew it. Harris Hanshue, by now convinced that it was feasible to fly over the Siskiyous since Gorst's pilots had been doing it daily for a year, offered to buy Gorst's B-shares, which controlled PAT, at a price that assured a nice profit for Gorst. But the deal would have left the pilots, suppliers, and investors, who owned 4,500 nonvoting A-shares, holding the sack. Gorst sought the advice of his new financial adviser. Patterson, whose decisions invariably are based on what is right rather than what is expedient, argued stoutly against accepting the Hanshue offer.

"Let's fly up to Seattle and see if we can't get some Boeings," he said.

Gorst, who had seen his unpaid financial aide pull rabbits out of the hat before, readily agreed. At the Seattle session, Patterson did pull a rabbit out of the hat. When the Boeing Airplane Company executives balked at selling the planes on credit, banker Patterson turned to William E. Boeing and asked, "Why don't you buy all of Pacific Air Transport's outstanding stock, voting and nonvoting alike, and add PAT to Boeing Air Transport?"

Boeing liked the idea. So did Philip G. Johnson, president of both Boeing Air Transport and Boeing Airplane Company. Both Boeing and Johnson were impressed with the integrity and enthusiasm of the young Wells Fargo officer. Boeing agreed to keep all of PAT's people on the payroll and to pay $200 per share for all of PAT's stock. When Boeing handed Gorst a $94,000 check for control of PAT, Patterson asked Gorst what he was going to do with the money.

"I'm going to buy a Boeing flying boat and start an airline to Alaska." Then he added, prophetically, "I guess a fool and his money are soon parted." Gorst did launch the farthest-north airline. He sought an airmail contract but lost out to Pan American Airways. Forced to fold up his Alaska airline, he operated a flying service for sportsmen for a time. But without his financial wizard to advise him, he lost the magic touch and eventually gave up flying machines for motor stages in Oregon. Meantime, Patterson, whom Gorst had inoculated with the flying virus, found himself inexorably swept up in the updraft of the exciting air transport game.

Shortly after the PAT sale, Boeing's president Philip G. Johnson telephoned Patterson at his Wells Fargo desk. A syndicate of Mexican business interests had offered BAT a license to fly the airmail south of the border. Could Patterson fly to Los Angeles, meet with the promoters and size up their proposal? As a favor to a depositor, Patterson did. He reported back to Johnson that the license to fly in Mexico was not a contract approved by the government and recommended against the risky venture. Johnson asked if he could fly up to Seattle. Patterson flew up on a Saturday afternoon. Johnson met him at the airport. They drove directly to Bill Boeing's house for dinner. Nobody mentioned the Mexican airmail deal. Patterson began to wonder why he was spending the weekend in Seattle instead of at home with his wife and baby daughter. After dinner, Johnson asked Patterson if he could stay over until Monday.

"I'd like to show you something tomorrow," he said.

On Sunday morning, Johnson took his still puzzled young guest down to the Boeing Airplane plant. Johnson pointed out the rows of planes under construction, then opened doors bearing big signs, "Secret Military Work—Keep Out." Finally they arrived at Johnson's office. Through an open door, Patterson could see another office furnished with a shiny new desk and chairs.

"This is my desk, and that is yours," said Johnson.

"My desk?" exclaimed Patterson.

"Yes, I need a right-hand man," replied Johnson. "You're just the fellow we need to bring some order into this business."

Patterson protested that he was doing right well at the Wells Fargo Bank, adding that he had just bought a new home in Piedmont, California.

"You'll do better up here," argued Johnson. "There's a phone. Call up your wife and see what she says."

After some discussion, Patterson did. An understanding wife, Vera Patterson allowed that she knew Pat would never be happy

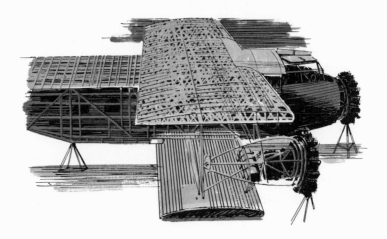

until he had had a go at the challenging air transport game. They could sell their new home and find another in Seattle. Patterson flew back to San Francisco Monday to report to the bank that he was resigning to accept the Boeing offer. President Lipman shook his head dubiously. He still held a gloomy view of the future of the flying machine business.

"I'll never be satisfied until I try it," insisted Patterson.

"Go ahead, then," said Lipman. "But your desk will be waiting if you want to come back to the bank any time within the next three years."

The following years were exciting and crucial in Patterson's career. On January 22, 1929, age 29, he moved to Seattle to plunge into the aviation game as assistant to Johnson who was president of both Boeing Airplane Company and Boeing Air Transport. Johnson was an airplane builder first, and an airline operator second. He was obliged to spend much time in Washington, D. C., the military market for Boeing's sleek, fast fighter planes. A big merger was in the works. Shy, retiring Bill Boeing and his friend, Frederick B. Rentschler, aggressive head of Pratt & Whitney of Hartford, Connecticut, which built the powerful Wasp engines, were putting together the country's first aviation giant, the United Aircraft and Transport Company. United would manufacture planes, engines and propellers, and operate a chain of five airlines to fly mail and passengers from coast to coast for the first time without a change of planes in Chicago. Phil Johnson, slated to head this new aviation giant, was in the east when Patterson reported for work at the Boeing Airplane plant early in 1929.

"He'll be away for five weeks," Johnson's secretary told Patterson. "He left some work and a note on your desk."

The somewhat nonplused assistant to the president found that his new boss had scooped up a stack of letters and memos and dumped them on the shiny Patterson desk with a note to make decisions as he saw fit. One immediate task was to track down owners of 4,500 nonvoting shares in Pacific Air Transport, which Patterson had persuaded Boeing to buy. Vern Gorst had swapped shares in lieu of money to pay pilots, station men, and suppliers.

The certificates were in lockers and desk drawers from Seattle to Los Angeles. When word got about that wealthy Bill Boeing was buying up all outstanding shares, the price of the once-worthless $100 par value shares skyrocketed. A Portland attorney had organized a syndicate of owners of the shares to hold out for all Boeing would pay. Patterson finally had to pay as much as $666 per share for them. He picked up the last two outstanding certificates from the shrewd madam of a North Bend, Oregon, house of masculine pleasure.

For the first year, the youthful banker turned flying machine man divided his energies about equally between airplane manufacturing and airline operating. Then, late in 1929, as the great depression was spreading like an economic fog across the country, a different type of catastrophe hit Boeing Air Transport.

BAT was the brainchild of Edward Hubbard, a World War I pilot and a flying pal of Bill Boeing. A decade before, in 1919, Eddie Hubbard had talked Canadian postal authorities into allowing him to fly mail bound for the Orient via Canadian Pacific steamer from Seattle to Victoria. This flight across Puget Sound, one of the first airmail services anywhere, saved a day for outgoing and incoming mail. Bill Boeing provided the airplane and sometimes flew it, to spell Hubbard. Hubbard, who also flew as test pilot for Boeing planes, learned through his Post Office connections that the Postmaster General planned to call for bids in January 1927 for the Chicago-San Francisco route. After a push from designer Claire Egtvedt, and later from Phil Johnson and Mrs. Boeing as well, reluctant Bill Boeing agreed to submit what proved to be the winning bid for the route. When the first 40-As came out of the Boeing plant, Eddie Hubbard launched Boeing Air Transport on July 1, 1927, with headquarters in Salt Lake City, junction of the airmail routes from Los Angeles, San Francisco, Seattle, and Chicago.

The catastrophe in the winter of 1929 was the loss of BAT's guiding genius. While strenuously shoveling snow in front of his house, Hubbard collapsed and died of a heart attack in the prime of life. This left the airline sector of the growing Boeing empire

Our Good Neighbor Policy

EVERY SO OFTEN *I ask myself, "What kind of a personality is United Air Lines?" Then I remind myself that we are corporate citizens in more than 100 cities along our system. We have the same civic and social obligations in each of them as do individual citizens. We are responsible for the impact which we make on the social and economic standards of each community we serve. This philosophy is accepted by our directors and our management and it permeates down through our organization. Our company accepts this responsibility and we expect all of our people to assume their share of the duty of making United Air Lines a good personality in every community in which we are a corporate citizen. We have had only commendation from our stockholders for adopting this basic philosophy. In fact, many new stockholders have told us that it was this conviction and its practical application that made our company an attractive investment to them.*

W.A.P.

without a head. When Phil Johnson looked around for a man to replace Hubbard his eye fell on Patterson.

"You have a new title," he told Patterson. "Executive vice president and general manager of Boeing Air Transport."

Thus, scarcely a year and a half after leaving the bank, Patterson was in charge of the country's largest and most profitable airline, with a fleet of 25 mail-passenger aircraft. He was doing all right in the flying machine business, despite the forebodings of his former banking associates at Wells Fargo. This was just the beginning. Before the year was up, the merger moves had added three more airlines to the United Aircraft empire. After a hot proxy battle, Frederick Rentschler acquired control of National Air Transport, which held the New York-Chicago airmail contract. Stout Air Services, flying out of Detroit, came into the fold, as did Varney Air Lines, connecting Salt Lake City with Spokane, Portland, and Seattle. Boeing already owned Pacific Air Transport. Patterson was made vice president and executive head of all of these airlines, except Stout, which was absorbed by National Air Transport. His chief, Phil Johnson, moved east to head the holding company, United Aircraft and Transport, with offices in New York City. Patterson's job was to make the day-to-day decisions and run the four airlines.

Some of these routine decisions had far-reaching repercussions in the air transport industry. One occurred early in 1930 when Patterson fielded a cryptic telegram from ebullient Steve Stimpson, San Francisco traffic manager for Boeing Air Transport. It read, "Stand by for important communication following by airmail." During a bumpy flight from Salt Lake City on BAT's newest tri-motor, 12-passenger luxury airliner, known as the 80-A, Stimpson had taken over the co-pilot's side chore of passing out sandwiches and pouring hot coffee from a thermos bottle and trying to reassure the queasy passengers as the plane jounced through storm clouds. When he reached his office, Stimpson urged his superiors to employ stewards aboard the 80-As. Given the go-ahead, Stimpson had already hired three "couriers" when a greater inspiration smote him.

Into Stimpson's office had walked an earnest young nurse from

San Francisco's French Hospital. Ellen Church had big dreams about becoming an airline pilot, but after some flying lessons she realized that flying an airliner was a man's job. As second choice, she proposed to Stimpson that Boeing Air Transport add a third member to the flying crew of each airliner. The third member would be a flying nurse who would take tickets, serve food, and keep the passengers comfortable and happy. Her two-hour visit sent Stimpson's imagination soaring. He immediately wired another W. A. Patterson, known as "Big Pat" because of his size, whose job was hiring crews for the planes. Back came a fast reply, "No." Stimpson decided to try the idea on "Little Pat," who was "Big Pat's" boss, but to use more of the vaunted Stimpson sales technique. The result was the "stand by" telegram to executive vice president Patterson in Seattle, followed by the important communication by airmail. It read:

"It strikes me that there would be a great psychological punch in having young women stewardesses or couriers, or whatever you want to call them, and I am certain that there are some mighty good ones available. I have in mind a couple of graduate nurses that would make exceptional stewardesses. Of course, it would be distinctly understood that there would be no reference made to their hospital training or nursing experience, but it would be a mighty fine thing to have this available, sub rosa, if necessary for air sickness.

"Imagine the psychology of having young women as regular members of the crew. Imagine the national publicity we could get from it, and the tremendous effect it would have on the traveling public. And imagine the value they would be to us not only in the neater and nicer methods of serving food but in looking out for the passengers' welfare."

Stimpson's enthusiasm failed to set BAT headquarters afire. President Phil Johnson, who happened to be in Seattle at the time, was cool to the idea. Flying crews who heard about the startling innovation vociferously allowed that they were too busy flying their planes to look after a helpless female in the crew. The decision was left to Patterson, who stuck Stimpson's memo in his pocket. The big hurdle to stimulating air traffic at the time was fear, mainly wives' fear of having their husbands travel by air. That evening, after his wife had finished feeding their infant daughter, Patty (who grew up to be a stewardess on a rival airline), he handed Stimpson's message to her and asked, "What do you think of this idea?"

Vera Patterson thought it was great. Her enthusiasm rekindled Patterson's. The next morning he talked some more with his colleagues at Boeing headquarters, concluding with, "I think we ought to give this a try."

"Okay, Pat," agreed Phil Johnson. "It's your baby."

Patterson called Steve Stimpson in San Francisco and told him to hire Ellen Church and seven other nurses, weighing not over 115 pounds apiece in their scanties and willing to fly 100 hours per month for $125 pay, plus expenses during layovers. Stimpson and Ellen Church were told to design suitable uniforms for the flying nurses. It was the flapper era and, fearful that Stimpson might go overboard on uniforms, Patterson cautioned, "We don't want a bunch of usherettes in pantaloons."

"I'm not suggesting at all the flapper type of girl," Stimpson assured him.

A few days later, Patterson flew to San Francisco to check the first corps of eight stewardesses, whom Stimpson and Ellen Church

An Employee's Job Is His Capital

L ET US CONSIDER *a man's—or a woman's—wage or salary, and ask ourselves, "How much principal would he need under existing interest rates to produce that much income for his family?" Let us assume that the figure arrived at is $50,000. Then, if you are thinking of discharging him, forget the man and say to yourself, "Here is an employee coming into my office and I am about to reach into his pocket and take out $50,000." We are always dealing in dollars and it is important to place a monetary value on the individual's job. If we do that we will automatically do some good healthy thinking in regard to him. It has always been helpful to me to measure the employee in terms of what his job is worth to him as capital. With this as a guide there is a greater effort to save a man than destroy him.*

W.A.P.

had rounded up by stalking the wards of San Francisco hospitals.

"Pat, we have been able to get uniforms for only three of the stewardesses," said Stimpson. "I'll bring the girls in."

When the trio came into the office, Patterson's face fell. They were blanketed like Amish women, with shapeless ground-sweeping skirts, drab capes, and bonnets. Stimpson waited for Patterson to recover, then said, "I've got five more girls upstairs, Pat. I'll bring them down."

The five were in the real stewardess uniforms, designed by Stimpson and Miss Church — dark green double-breasted jackets and skirts, long green capes with gray collars, green tams shaped like shower caps — a far cry from the chic stewardess costumes of later years. But in 1930, they looked real snappy to Patterson and to the delighted air travelers whom they greeted at the doorways of the 80-A luxury airliners.

Lacking a training school for the new profession, Ellen Church and the first flying airwomen learned as they flew how to serve meals, take tickets, keep passengers happy, and sell air travel. Pilots quickly changed from skeptics to boosters; they could forget about passengers and concentrate on flying their planes. They also enjoyed having chicken and coffee served in the cockpits. Before the trial period ended, Patterson instructed chief stewardess Church to recruit a score more nurses and to plan a training course. Soon, other airlines also hired stewardesses. Before long, thousands of young women were flying the airlines of the world as members of crews. During World War II, when nurses were needed for more important duty, the nursing requirement was dropped.

At United, the BAT original eight grew into a stewardess staff of over 3,000 by 1965. Every year at least 1,500 "sky girls" graduated from the United training school to take the places of those grounded largely by Cupid. For a period the United stewardess service was a Gretna Green on wings. The average stewardess flew 13 months before becoming a bride; later the average stewardess career stabilized at around 30 months. The "Clipped Wings," as United's grounded former stewardesses call themselves, now number over 1,200 wives, many of them mothers of bright-eyed smiling new sky girls. Patterson's decision in 1930, with the timely nudge from his wife, unexpectedly made him godfather to a profession for more than 100,000 young women in three-score lands.

Fred Rentschler and Bill Boeing, the moving spirits behind the United Aircraft and Transport holding company, had a somewhat unworkable theory that the several companies under the United umbrella were "joined together" to help each other rather than "hammered together" on a financial anvil. Headquarters for United Aircraft and Transport were in New York City, but the airlines and the airplane builders ran their own shows as almost autonomous businesses. It soon became apparent that this was not practical or efficient for the four airlines. Together they made up the largest air transport system anywhere at the time. They had more flying know-how, having flown over 40 million flight miles, half of them at night. They carried over half of the country's air cargo and passengers, 43,928 air travelers in 1931. The United group crystallized Postmaster General Walter F. Brown's ideal of an airline that flew "from somewhere to somewhere."

At the time, the nation was crisscrossed with spoonfed small airmail contract lines that flew between two or more cities. Under the McNary-Watres Act, the Postmaster General was authorized to modify the rate structure of these little airlines which ultimately paved the way for merger into transcontinental lines rivalling the United system. The goal was to get the air transport industry off the government subsidy as soon as possible. On May 19, 1930, Postmaster General Walter F. Brown called a conference of all airmail contract carriers in Washington, D. C. to twist arms and push them into mergers. Out of the conference came three new transcontinental systems that soon captured almost half of the airmail business of the four airlines in the United fold. By rare good luck, Patterson was not invited to this conference in Washington. He was busy in Seattle running BAT and PAT. By equally rare bad luck, Phil Johnson did attend the meeting, mainly as a spectator to mergers that boded no good for the United airways system.

During 1930, it had become evident that Seattle was not the place from which to run a transcontinental airline. Neither was

New York, where United Aircraft and Transport had set up the holding company executive headquarters, first at 51 Pine Street, close to the Wall Street financial mart, later at 230 Park Avenue. The United top management decided to have the airlines' operating base in Chicago, where a new corporation, United Air Lines, Incorporated, would serve as the catalyst for gradually welding the four lines into one system. At the start, United Air Lines was to be the traffic-getter for the four. Each airline was a separate unit. Phil Johnson was president of United Air Lines, as well as titular head of each of the airlines. Busy selling airplanes and engines to the Army and Navy, and working on additional mergers, he left the running of the airlines to his man Friday.

Patterson moved from Seattle to Chicago in 1931 and opened a head office for United Air Lines, BAT, NAT, PAT, and Varney Air Lines in the La Salle-Wacker Building. He was executive vice president of all five companies, and president of the latter four companies after July 1, 1933. He was rocketing ahead in the flying machine game. Luckily, he had three good years — '31, '32, and '33 — even though they were at the bottom of the great depression, to jell his ideas of how to run an airline before facing up to the most crucial test of his mettle in 1934.

CHAPTER III

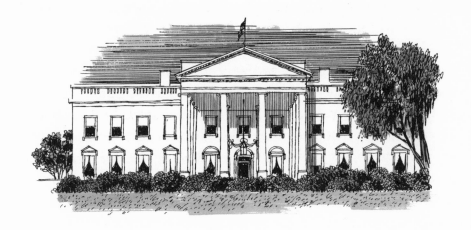

Most Momentous Decision

In the penetrating, dark brown eyes of the youthful head of the four closely affiliated airlines making up the country's largest airways system, the glamour boys were the dashing pilots in trim gray uniforms who flew the airliners. One of the few top airline executives who was not a former pilot, Patterson idolized fliers. Consequently, it came as a real shocker to learn late in 1933 that his heroes on NAT had voted to strike on November 26 to back up their demands for more pay and better flying rules. Inexperienced in labor negotiations, Patterson sought the advice of older employers.

"Don't let your employees tell you how to run your business," they told him.

Acting on this counsel, Patterson made plans to keep as many planes aloft as possible with non-union flight crews. He was in New York wrestling with emergency operating measures when a phone call came in from Newark Airport, eastern terminus of the

United chain. Three veteran pilots who had been flying the New York-Chicago route since before NAT had taken over the airmail carrying wanted to know if he would come out to the airport and listen to their side of the dispute.

"Sure I will," he agreed. "I'll come out right away."

It was late evening when he joined the pilots, who had flown the mail for the Post Office and who had joined NAT when it won the New York-Chicago contract in 1927. In the all-night session that followed, the veteran fliers laid it on the line before their chief. They told how they had risked their lives to help get the airmail service started, how they had struggled along on low wages, both from the Post Office and later from thriving National Air Transport. They resented flying orders given by non-fliers at the ground stations and cited the difficult and haphazard family life they were forced to live, always on call even on their days off. Their demand for more pay and better working conditions took on a new light in Patterson's concept. Along about sunrise, the weary young president admitted that his eyes had been opened.

"I've learned something tonight," he told the pilots. "I think you fellows are 90 percent right and the company is 90 percent wrong. Let's submit our wage and hour differences to an arbitrator. Meantime, I'll go over the whole system and talk with every pilot personally. I'll settle most of your grievances on the spot."

The fliers accepted this offer and persuaded their union to call off the strike. Patterson spent the next two months out on the line, talking day and night with pilots and co-pilots as their planes arrived at airports. Tossing the advice of elders to the wind, he invited every employee he met to tell him how to run the airline. He returned to Chicago headquarters with a head full of new ideas and a slant on labor relations which soon came to be known in the growing United fold as "the personal touch with employees." Patterson resolved to spend half of each year out on the line inviting suggestions from every worker he could contact face to face. At each airport, the gregarious young president, who genuinely enjoyed swapping thoughts with people, gathered employees around a counter or a bench and opened up with, "I've come to talk some company problems over with you, but first let's take up your own problems."

Patterson has said repeatedly since then, "That's how I learned the airline business — from our people." He means it, too.

His talk on company problems included candid answers to anything any employee wanted to know about the airline. His talks with the pilots had persuaded him that employees had a right to know how much the company was making, or losing, who owned or controlled it, how much top executives were paid, what the airline paid for planes, how to win promotions, or anything else about the United companies. There was a purpose behind this candor. He wanted every worker to feel that the airline was his, the employee's, airline. Also, he had hit on an effective public relations device: informed employees could give intelligent answers about the airline.

Before he could carry out his personal-touch program, the Patterson talkfest with people was interrupted temporarily by a bolt out of the blue from Washington, D. C. On February 9, 1934, five identical telegrams arrived from Postmaster General James A. Farley. Four were addressed to him as the four-hat president of NAT, BAT, PAT, and Varney Air Lines, the fifth to the vice president of United Air Lines. Farley was summarily cancelling all airmail contracts, not only with the four United companies but with all airmail contractors throughout the country, effective midnight of February 19. By presidential decree, the airmail was to be flown by U. S. Army pilots after that date. This astounding ukase led to one of Patterson's most momentous decisions, one that probably saved not only United Air Lines but the entire air transport industry as well for private enterprise.

Patterson's unquenchable sense of humor helped absorb the shock of the catastrophic news. He was in a deep huddle with other executives trying to decide whether or not to spend a few thousand dollars on two spare Wasp engines when the five telegrams were delivered. Before they could be opened, Bob Johnson, United's publicity man, burst in on the conference and exploded, "Pat, the AP just called about a flash from Washington that our airmail contracts are cancelled. They want to know what we have to say about it."

"Well, gentlemen," laughed Patterson, "That settles our engine problem."

The abrupt cancellation swept almost half of United's revenue out the window. For other airlines with less passenger business it was even more devastating. The phones began to ring like mad. Other airline operators wanted to know what Patterson proposed to do. If United, the strongest airline, ceased flying, the entire industry might fold. Air transport could become a government monopoly in the United States as it was — and still is — in nearly all other countries.

Patterson decided that he had to get out of the madhouse to have time and quiet to think the cataclysmic turn of events through. He put on his hat and left the office. Early that afternoon, he called Bob Johnson to his home.

"We're going to continue all operations," he said. "We're not going to cancel any flights or lay off anybody. I'll phone our chief pilots and station managers and tell them to keep on flying. You call the press and the other airline operators and tell them our decision."

Other airlines curtailed schedules or closed down completely. Patterson's determination to fly all schedules, without mail revenue and with too few fares, cost the companies he headed more than $1 million in the three months that followed. But Patterson still rates it as one of the soundest decisions he ever made.

With apprehensive employees assured their paychecks and United's 60 new 247s on the wing, Patterson hustled to Washington, D. C. to see what, if anything, could be salvaged from the wreck of the airways. He found that nearly all of the heads of the country's many little airlines that had lost airmail contracts were already there. So were a host of barnstormers waiting like hopeful buzzards to pick up, if possible, the contracts the pioneer operators had lost.

Patterson found that the abrupt cancellation by the Postmaster General was an order from the White House. President Franklin D. Roosevelt chose to label the May 19, 1930 meeting called in Washington by Postmaster General Brown, "the spoils conference," at which the airline operators were supposedly in collusion to divide up the Post Office airmail contracts. Despite the fact that he had been merely a reluctant spectator to the mergers that created two lusty transcontinental rivals who were cutting deeply into United's earnings, United's president Phil Johnson was tagged as a "collusionist," too. Only the good luck that he happened to be in Seattle at the time saved Patterson from being smeared.

The government action soon boomeranged. The Army Air Corps had ten days in which to assemble 160 observation and bomber planes and a force of 200 pilots to fly them. The army pilots, trained in acrobatic flying, were no match for the fierce winter weather when they took over as airmail pilots on February 19, 1934. Weather-wise, February of that year was the most hazardous on record for airmail flying. By the end of the first week, five pilots had been killed and six more critically injured in crashes which smashed up $500,000 worth of Army planes. Patterson sent out orders to United's pilots, station managers, and ground crews to help the hapless Army fliers in any way possible. But pilots continued to drop out of stormy skies. Nine crashed on the United Main Line routes alone.

Responding to outraged public protests, President Roosevelt

abruptly cancelled all airmail flying after three weeks of disaster. When the Army pilots resumed service on March 17, they flew only by day. Letters that United's pilots had carried from San Francisco to New York in 19 hours now took 48 hours to cross the country. Irate airmail users made up packets of letters in San Francisco, Chicago, and New York, dispatched them by United air express, to be mailed at the opposite ends of the Main Line. On March 30, after six calamitous weeks, the President yielded to Postmaster General Farley's pleas. The Post Office called for new airmail bids.

The airline presidents, most of them staying at the Carlton Hotel about two blocks from the White House, decided to seek an interview with President Roosevelt. They were soon rewarded with an invitation to the White House for Patterson. This had its humorous side. Patterson received a surprise phone call one morning at his hotel.

"This is Miss LeHand," said the caller. "The President would like you to have dinner with him tonight at the White House."

Patterson thanked "Miss LeHand," then dismissed the call from his mind, suspecting that one of his rivals was up to a prank. About midafternoon, a newspaper reporter braced him and said, "I see you're on the list of guests to dine at the White House tonight. What's it all about?"

"You're kidding," replied Patterson.

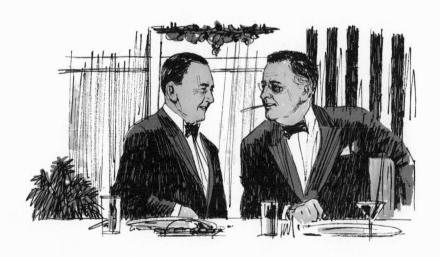

"I'm not kidding at all. Your name's on the posted dinner guest list."

"I don't even have a dinner suit with me," protested Patterson.

"You'd better hustle out and rent one," advised the newsman.

Patterson checked the rent-a-suit haberdashers. Not one had a dinner suit in his size. One agreed to remodel a suit in a hurry if Patterson would buy it. He bought the suit, with shirt, tie, and cuff links, to be delivered to his hotel, where the word had gone around about his invitation to the White House. The other airline men were sure that the President had chosen Patterson to convey a message to them. His new dinner suit arrived barely in time for him to slip into it and catch a taxi to the White House.

"Front door or side door?" asked the taxi driver.

"Let's go right in the front door," said Patterson.

Secret Service men escorted him into the Red Room, where he met several other guests. Miss LeHand, the President's secretary, escorted them into the private dining room, where Patterson was seated at the host's left. The President, in an expansive mood, talked of the paintings he had bought for $25 that were now worth $5,000 apiece but failed to give Patterson clearance for any words about the airlines' plight. When the dinner ended, F.D.R. singled him out and said, "Pat, won't you come up to my study with me?" On the way to the study, he turned to his secretary and asked, "Missy, what do we have in the way of movies tonight?"

"David Copperfield," she replied.

It was a long movie, ending at 10:45. As the lights came on, Patterson saw Miss LeHand holding a stack of letters to be signed.

"Mr. President, I've enjoyed the evening," he said.

"Pat, I've enjoyed it, too." replied Roosevelt. "Will you come and see me again?"

Back at the Carlton Hotel, Patterson found the other airline presidents sitting on chairs around a big room, with one in the middle for him. They waited impatiently while he downed a drink. His report was brief.

"I had a wonderful evening, but I'm not sure the President knew what business I'm in," he said.

The following Saturday evening, back home, he and his wife were going to a dinner party.

"I might as well wear my new dinner suit," he said.

When he appeared dressed for the party, Vera Patterson asked, "Whose suit are you wearing?"

"It's mine. The one I bought for my dinner at the White House."

"Look at yourself in the mirror," she said

One look convinced Patterson that the Washington haberdasher had not altered the suit at all. It was much too large for him. He changed back into an old dinner suit. The next day Good Will Industries was richer by one new dinner suit.

Patterson soon found himself facing another perplexing decision. The Post Office had been paying around 54 cents per plane mile for carrying the airmail. The Army's cost had soared to $2.21 per plane mile. Washington hotels were full of airplane owners eager to bid low to get airmail contracts, hoping for adjustments later if and when they lost their flying shirts. Patterson sharpened his pencil and submitted bids that would allow United's planes to make a fair return. He won back all of the United companies' contracts, with the exception of the Chicago-Dallas route, at 39.5 cents per plane mile. United was back in the airmail carrying business again, at a profit. Most rivals had bid so low they were carrying the mail at a loss.

Recovery of the airmail contracts marked another leap upward in Patterson's spectacular rise as a flying machine man. One White House edict, backed later by a clause in the new airmail act enacted by Congress, decreed that no airline whose head had attended the mythical spoils conference could even bid on Post Office contracts. This arbitrary decree meant that every established airline had to be reorganized under a new name with a new chief executive. It banished Phil Johnson and nearly every other pioneer airline president for five years. United Air Lines, Incorporated became United Air Lines Transport Corporation, whose president, quite naturally, was William A. Patterson, the eager young beaver who had been the operating head of NAT, BAT, PAT, and Varney previous to

Communicating with People

IF YOU'RE TRYING *to persuade somebody, you'd better put your message in terms he can understand. That's why, when I talk to people, I try to do it at a level where I'm talking with them, rather than at them. I know what goes through the hearts and minds of people fighting for existence because I've been through these experiences. I can put myself in the other fellow's boots. I recall coming into Philadelphia one blustery day when a gust of wind caught our plane as a mechanic was taxiing it away from the terminal and turned it on its nose. Someone said, "That poor fellow is going to die a thousand deaths." So, rather than let him lie awake all night, I asked them to bring him into the airport office to see me. He was shaking all over, so I said, "Don't worry. I've seen pilots do that," and slapped him on the back. You could see the relief come over him. I've had things like that happen to me and a kind word has saved my feelings. So I always ask myself, "Do I want to make that fellow a better man as the result of the accident or do I want him to go out of my office with his fists clenched and his heart bitter?" My answer is that I want him to go out vowing that he'll never let me down. Then I know that airplane is safer in his hands than in any other mechanic's.*

W.A.P.

the cancellation. The four airlines were quickly merged into the new United Air Lines Transport Corporation. Another decree split up the aviation holding companies that controlled both airlines and airplane manufacturing plants. Still another rule arbitrarily limited salaries of executives of airlines holding airmail contracts to $17,500 a year.

Thus on July 20, 1934, at 34 years of age, Patterson moved into the president's chair of the country's largest airline. He had 6,000 miles of airline and a fleet of 60 Boeing 247s, the last word in airliners at the moment. He was on his own, completely unshackled from the United Aircraft and the Boeing Airplane managements. He was responsible only to 23,000 scattered stockholders, no one of whom owned over one percent of the airline's shares. His sponsor, Joseph Pierce Ripley, the New York financial genius who had unscrambled in one month the aviation holding company he had put together five years before, chose a United Air Lines directorship rather than membership on the board of either United Aircraft Company or Boeing Airplane Company. With canny foresight, Ripley saw that the airline got the big bite of the former holding company's working capital. Patterson started his presidency with $4 million cash in banks along the airline. Even more important, he inherited a staff of veterans in their early forties, many of whom had been pilots since flying postmen days. They were the most experienced management team employed by any airline anywhere. With rough flying weather ahead, the youngest airline president, who had never flown a plane himself, knew that he needed these millions and these men.

"With the right men behind you, you're bound to look pretty good," he says, looking back at this milestone in his career.

Like Patterson, most of the country's fresh crop of airline heads owed their presidencies to the airmail purge. Glad to have their airmail contracts and even more delighted to be top executives, they were willing to forgive and forget and let bygones be bygones. But Patterson wasn't. To him, right is right and wrong is wrong. His former chief, Phil Johnson, who had pioneered the airline business, had been wronged. Johnson took the wrong in stride and served willingly as one of the committee of three headed by Joe Ripley that worked out the reorganization of the United Aircraft and Transport empire. But Patterson brooded over it and determined that somehow Johnson must be vindicated of any wrongdoing.

About the only means of vindication, except by public opinion, was to bring suit in federal courts. The United States Supreme Court refused to consider a suit to clear Johnson of collusion charges. But the U. S. Court of Claims accepted a suit by PAT and BAT to recover $3,100,555.43 in postal revenues allegedly lost by the arbitrary airmail cancellation. Winning this suit, to Patterson's way of thinking, would imply vindication for Johnson. It dragged out for years, and became known as "the long suit." A token award to United was finally handed down in 1943, by which time Phil Johnson had long since vindicated himself by building Trans-Canada Airlines (now Air Canada) and by returning to his old position as head of Boeing Airplane Company, to spark the phenomenal wartime production of Flying Fortresses. But to Patterson this token victory meant vindication for Johnson.

Repeatedly Patterson's friends in Washington urged him to call off the long suit. He stubbornly refused. "We could see United's problems more clearly if smoke didn't get in our eyes," a high Post Office official told him. United's applications for new route certificates languished, while rival American Airlines and Trans World Airlines added routes into 60 population centers, including a number formerly served only by United. By 1937, Patterson's most formidable rival, C. R. Smith, had added so many traffic centers to his system that American was the country's Number 1 airline and United was Number 2. Frustrated and convinced that he was in the doghouse for good in Washington, Patterson attempted to even the score by buying smaller airlines or by merging them into the United network. He managed to put United into Denver by buying the Cheyenne-Denver leg of Wyoming Air Service. He almost succeeded in invading the Detroit, Milwaukee, and Washington, D. C. traffic meccas by taking over Pennsylvania-Central Airlines, a merger that was blocked at the last minute by other financial interests — until a quarter century later when Capital Airlines, successor to Pennsylvania-Central Airlines, came into the United fold.

In the years of bumpy flying that followed "the purge," Patterson adopted an attitude toward Roosevelt's highhanded and arbitrary shake up of the emerging air transport industry that was an oil-water blend of ire and pragmatism. At 35, he was an old-timer among airline heads and their outspoken champion. In talks before business groups, he philosophically accepted the purge as "a spanking that made us better boys."

"Although a terrific jolt to the companies and unfair to individuals," he declared, "the cancellations were a blessing in disguise because they stopped the financial manipulations of the earlier era and saved the airlines from the long period of speculation and consequent receiverships that the railroads went through."

Its defiant president determined that the reorganized United Air Lines Transport Corporation must become independent of federal airmail subsidy as quickly as possible. Under his constant prodding, United's passenger and cargo agents rustled up new business in every traffic center served by the airlines' planes, sometimes with amusing results. Winging up and down the airway, he urged everybody on the payroll, from managers to janitors, to think up new ways to help United earn more non-airmail revenues. Ideas poured in. One of the happiest brainstorms bubbled out of Steve Stimpson, the creative San Francisco traffic agent who had fathered the stewardess ten-strike.

"Why not invite our male passengers to take their wives along free on business trips?" proposed Stimpson, who had been watching United's 247s take off day after day with half their seats empty. "It would cost us practically nothing to have a wife occupying an empty seat."

At the time the big hurdle to filling the planes was fear of air travel, particularly fear on the part of wives who wanted their husbands on the ground, not up in the air.

"Try it out between San Francisco and Los Angeles," Patterson told Stimpson.

The tryout proved so successful that within three weeks Patterson extended the take-your-wife-free offer to the busy Chicago-New York run. On one day, 68 wives flew with husbands between these two cities. With this key to developing new business, Patterson put the plan into effect over the entire United system. Other airlines adopted the idea and before long there were almost as many women as men in the airliners. Patterson assumed they were wives — until returns began to come in from a cheery follow-up letter Stimpson got out to venturesome spouses telling them how it delighted United Air Lines to have them aboard. Then it developed that frequently a husband neglected to tell his wife he had taken her along on a business trip as the guest of the airline.

The drive for traffic paid off in passenger and cargo traffic more lucrative than carrying airmail at the skimpy rates paid by the Post Office under the new contracts. Within two years, by 1936, two out of every three dollars generated by United's planes came from passenger and cargo revenues. Cargo was stacked in the front seats of the 247s; it rode as comfortably as the passengers. Patterson began to visualize an airliner with compartments below the floor for luggage and cargo. He had negotiated a contract with Railway Express to pick up and deliver express shipments for 12.5 cents out of every dollar of revenue collected for flying packages across the country. This deal put him at loggerheads with the rest of the air transport industry. Rival airlines organized their own air express company, operating their own pick-up and delivery service in the larger traffic centers. After two years of footing the bills, they were ready to join United in a blanket contract with Railway Express, still in effect after three decades.

At the diluted rates paid by the Post Office for flying the airpost, the airmail contracts soon ceased to be subsidy for the major airlines. They flew the mail at a handsome profit for the Post Office, which used the earnings to subsidize numerous local airlines between small cities. Patterson rated this discrimination as a blessing in disguise, too. It forced United and its growing transcontinental rivals to hustle harder for passengers. But he delighted in twitting Post Office, Interstate Commerce Commission, and later Civil

Aeronautics Board officials for glaring examples of spoon-feeding, such as the subsidy by which two Pacific Coast local lines were paid $30 per ton for carrying mail for which United received 68 cents over the same route.

During the thirties, the federal government whip over the airlines changed hands from the Post Office to the Interstate Commerce Commission to the newly organized Civil Aeronautics Authority in 1938. Quite independently, the Civil Aviation Agency operated airways beacons, spurred the building of airports, and wrote the rules for flying the planes. Each time the whip changed hands, an interminable round of hearings took place in Washington to educate a new graduating class of government bureaucrats. During the five years that the Interstate Commerce Commission policed the airlines as a sideline to railroad regulations, decisions came more slowly than the proverbial slow train through Arkansas.

Other airlines added Washington representatives to their staffs to cut through the tangle of red tape. Patterson chose to be his own Washington spokesman. He and other United staffers journeyed to Washington time after time to tell the United story in person, or to plead for route extensions. Eventually he concluded that his safaris into the Washington jungle to bag new routes or protect those United already flew were not paying off. He reached into the District of Columbia Public Utilities Commission and hired a witty and aggressive attorney, James Francis Reilly, to serve as United's Washington counsel. Reilly came well qualified, having been executive assistant to the chairman of the CAB and an examiner at the Board. The big and bombastic Irishman, and Patterson, the short and encyclopaedic president, made a picturesque and effective team at congressional, CAB, and CAA hearings. They blasted bureaucratic rulings and Rip Van Winkle inactivity with forthright candor, yet managed to command the respect of the officials they needled. Out of these experiences grew the unusual Patterson outlook on why we are regulated.

"I've seen many of these regulatory agencies — the CAB, the FAA, the SEC, the FTC and other alphabet bodies — come into being," he has said. "Unless the causes of their origin are under-

Humility in High Places

I'VE ALWAYS *considered it a tribute, one that I cherish highly, that people on all levels of our business have called me by my first name. When I've gone through our shops and mechanics have said, "Hello, Pat," it has always made me feel good. The attitude of importance that comes over some men when they become top executives has always annoyed me. Too often the president's job is the loneliest and least secure in a company. If there is anything important about me, I'm the last person to see it. I once received a rather glowing award from a university; when it came time to thank them for it, I just thanked them for overlooking my faults.*

W.A.P.

stood, there will be more. Grousing about the loss of liberty will not cause restrictive government agencies to go away. I've concluded that the moral from their existence is this: when you abuse liberty, you lose liberty. Trace the events that led to the origin of a restrictive agency and you invariably find that a few men interpreted liberty as the right to do as they pleased, without regard to ethics or to the interests of others. Their operations antagonized the public and Congress took action. It's as simple as that."

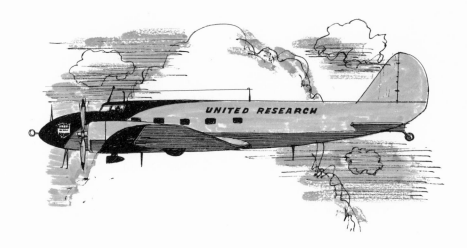

CHAPTER IV

The Rule of Five

Patterson took the loss of United's Number 1 position in the air transport industry to rival American Airlines with outward equanimity, contending that he would "rather run the best airline than the biggest." Rivals have twitted him about this "sour grapes" attitude, but with Patterson it was the real thing. He began his presidency as head of the biggest airline and later recouped, eventually retiring as boss of the world's largest airliner fleet, with his point of view unchanged—he'd rather be best than biggest.

For a former banker, his idea of being best was unorthodox. To Patterson, "best" didn't mean making the biggest profit. He thought in terms of what he characterized, with a typical Patterson flair for slogans, as the "Rule of Five." This was a guideline he coined shortly after he became president, and after United had been plagued by a series of accidents. Competitors had launched a whispering campaign to spread foggy doubt about the reliability of the Boeing 247s which only United was flying at the time. To demonstrate that the first all-metal airliner was a sturdy vehicle, Patterson delivered a stock 247 to the Army's military testing center, at Dayton, Ohio, where test pilots literally flew the plane into the ground to prove its structural strength.

Then, to make sure that United's pilots were as stout as their planes, he wrote out three rules for flying the 247s — Safety, Passenger Comfort, Dependability. Later, he added two more rules to the code — Honesty and Sincerity — and made his Rule of Five the bible for everyone who worked for United Air Lines. Every morning his staffers met in brief "flight plan" huddles to review the previous 24 hours' operations on the airline. At these and other employee meetings, Patterson plugged the Rule of Five with such fervor that it became literally the gospel of the airline. His faith in this gospel pulled him through some rough and dark periods in United's early history.

One rugged era grew out of the 1933 decision of the New York top echelon of the holding company to give the four United companies a monopoly of the sleek ten-passenger all-metal 247s built by its subsidiary, Boeing Airplane Company. After the unmerger, Patterson was free to buy airliners from any plane builder. But he was stuck with 60 of the 247s, which represented an investment of $4 million. He had to fly them to get the airline's money back, even after rival TWA and American Airlines introduced a new and better airliner, the DC-3, by up-and-coming Douglas Aircraft Com-

pany of Santa Monica, California. The DC-3s flew 25 miles faster than United's 247s and they carried 21 instead of 10 passengers. The DC-3s flew the heavy traffic New York-Chicago route nonstop in less than five hours, while United's 247s, which had to stop in Cleveland for refueling, took six hours or more. Fickle, time-minded passengers switched by the thousands from United to TWA and American.

Patterson faced a hard choice. He could dip deep into his $4 million reserve for a fleet of DC-3s, or he could dip into it for only $1 million to soup up the fleet of 247s. He chose the latter course, in a decision he soon regretted. With more powerful engines and new three-blade propellers, the 247s achieved a speed of 180 miles per hour, almost that of the DC-3s. But they still had to refuel in Cleveland and other way stations on the western routes, and they still carried only ten passengers. In a last-ditch effort to lure United's passengers back, he stepped up departures in both New York and Chicago to every hour on the hour. The cream of the traffic still rode rivals' DC-3s.

Patterson knew he was licked. In 1936, he bought a fleet of 22 of the DC-3s from Douglas at a cost of $2,400,000 to replace the outmoded 247s, which were sold or leased to other lines. This expensive battle for passengers taught the young flying machine man a lesson he never forgot, namely, that today's airliner, no matter how new, may be obsolete tomorrow. Never again was he caught without a faster plane on the drawing boards of United's engineering division.

Delivery of United's DC-3s late in 1936 opened a new phase in the tussle for passengers, particularly on the blue-ribbon New York-Chicago route. To lure fares back from TWA and American, Patterson tried "sky lounge" service, a 14-passenger deluxe cabin with swivel chairs, and a $2 extra fare, that sped between the nation's two top traffic centers in three hours, forty-five minutes. The sky lounge turned out to be a plushy flop. Passengers grumbled about the $2 extra fare, which put $28 into United's treasury for each full load, but lost seven full fares. Before the year was up, the sky lounges were converted into coast-to-coast DC-3 sleepers, with berths resembling those in Pullman cars, but with soft, light blankets, and linen sheets. It was the stewardesses' turn to grumble, as they wrestled with berths and tried to talk passengers into undressing and going to bed, just as on Pullman trains down below. Few passengers did. They objected to being awakened prior to each refueling landing to keep their eardrums from popping. Most of them wanted to have their shoes on if the airliner made a forced landing. Within a few months, "Sleep Your Way from San Francisco to New York" was only another lost horizon. The DC-3s again had 21 seats and the new inducement for passengers, aside from dependable service, was the best food in the sky.

United's first flight kitchen, and the first launched by any airline anywhere, opened in Oakland, California, early in 1937. It came about largely because Patterson, in his travels up and down the line, had eaten so much creamed and fried chicken that he sometimes suspected, like other steady United passengers, that he might be sprouting wings. He was discussing this lack of variety in airliner meals one day with a San Francisco hotel man.

"We just had a firm of hotel experts working on easier ways to give better dining service," said the hotel man. "Maybe they could do something for you."

Patterson's letter to the hotel experts landed on the desk of one of the junior partners, Don F. Magarrell, a Cornell-trained food and dining service expert. Magarrell promptly assigned himself to make a study for United. He soon demonstrated that he had chosen the right man for the job. After riding United airliners from one end of the system to the other and stopping over in all major terminals to check where the delicious fried chicken came from, Magarrell wound up in Santa Monica. There, Douglas and United engineers were trying to figure out a more efficient location for the food galleys than up front in the cabin which could be reached only by carrying the dinners up the narrow aisle from the door in the rear. Magarrell advised them to relocate the food and refreshment galleys on both sides of the airliner's entrance where larger thermal containers already packed for ready service could be hoisted aboard in a few minutes. This simple innovation revolutionized the food service not only on United planes but on those of other airlines.

Next, Magarrell made a report to Patterson pointing out that the deluxe dinners United bought from caterers at different terminals were pretty well undeluxed by the time they were jounced from downtown kitchens to the airports. "United ought to have its own flight kitchens in major terminals," urged Magarrell. "They'd soon pay for themselves not only in better meals but in reduced food costs."

"How much would it cost to try out the idea?" asked Patterson.

Magarrell thought he could set up an experimental flight kitchen at Oakland Airport, then the western terminus of the Main Line, for $3,000. This looked like such a bargain that Patterson told him to go ahead. For chef, Magarrell employed a Swiss, John Dietschy. The meals that Dietschy turned out made a hit with passengers. A flood of appreciative letters led Patterson to authorize flight kitchens in major terminals. Chef Dietschy had a Swiss chef friend who had another Swiss chef friend and before long United had a small army of Swiss chefs preparing meals at the major airports served by the company. The meticulous Swiss rose to the challenge of preparing plain dishes that squeamish stomachs could handle at abnormal altitudes and of making them look and taste like gourmet meals. The ingenious Swiss could think little and put together a square meal that was enough but not too much when served in cramped space between airliner seats.

To make sure that a passenger didn't eat Swiss steak for lunch and again for dinner on the same day, Magarrell evolved menus printed a month ahead of time for each flight kitchen. Stewardesses handed these neat menus out to whet passengers' appetites and to advise that "le serviette au cou might save a spot or two," if the diner wished to tuck his napkin Swiss-style under his chin. A perfectionist himself, Patterson idolized his perfectionist Swiss chefs almost as much as his perfectionist pilots. Once a year he gathered them at a posh hotel or club in a different United city to prepare a gourmet dinner for a top brass list of guests, including presidents, bankers, civic leaders. As each course was served, the Swiss chef who dreamed it up was introduced and cheered. Patterson as host invariably recalled the flight back in 40-B days when weather forced his plane to land at Reno about dinner time. He and his two cash customers were hungry. He asked the station manager to scrounge some food. The manager came back with some soggy sandwiches and two catsup bottles filled with hot coffee.

"Is this the way we serve coffee?" Patterson asked.

"What's the matter? Is it cold?" asked the station manager, solicitously.

Patterson concluded his talk with, "That's when I began to think about food service for our passengers. If they were flying at meal time, they were our guests, just as much as if they were in my home. We first tried a Harvey House type of quick lunch counter at Cheyenne, but the passengers preferred to kibitz the servicing of the planes during the stopover. When they got aboard they were hungry. So that's what led to our flight kitchens headed by these fine chefs. Last year they cost us over $10 million but it's one of the best buys we ever made."

While he was styling United's food service, Magarrell, who later became vice-president in charge of passenger service, began with Patterson's blessing, to spruce up United's planes, which were rechristened Mainliners and redecorated in pastel decor. A brave man, Magarrell even undertook to re-style the stewardesses, whose training was extended to five weeks at a school first in Cheyenne, later in Chicago. This stewardess-styling was so successful — or vice versa, depending upon the viewpoint — that at one time the average career of a United sky girl was but 13 months, after which she was grounded by marriage and the airline had to train another stewardess to take her place. Though this short tenure in uniform was expensive, Patterson rated it too as a good investment. "Our stewardesses are always eager and they don't get tired of their work," he insisted. His concern for the welfare of the sky girls has exceeded his paternal interest in any other group in the United family.

This concern was dramatized in 1954 when American and TWA decided to serve drinks on their luxurious new DC-7s. Patterson felt that it was a mistake to serve liquor on planes — and still

The Two Pay Windows

UNITED HAS TWO PAY *windows. The employees' pay window has always been open. If it should close, the employees would naturally quit. The stockholders' window is open only part of the time. Unless we keep that window open, our stockholders will quit and invest their money elsewhere.*

W.A.P.

What Is Security?

SECURITY IS SOMETHING *that must be earned, to mean anything. Unearned security makes us slaves of the dispenser, which nowadays is usually the government. That kind of security is subject to the whims of the bureaucrats who happen to be in power. Real security is a two-way street and you are not going to get it for nothing. In business, a company has an obligation to be conscious of every employee's security, but real security comes in the performance of his duties.*

W.A.P.

does — but his main objection was that he didn't want his stewardesses to become bar maids. After agonizing over the problem and recognizing that United had to meet the competition, he decreed, "We will not sell drinks, but we'll serve them as hospitality."

Magarrell worked out a smooth sequence in the food service whereby the passenger found himself with a juicy steak or a boned squab challenging his appetite about the time he finished his second highball. To Patterson's elastic thinking, this meant that the stewardess who had served the drinks was somebody's darling daughter helping out with the hospitality — perhaps his own, as he discovered to his surprise one day when his arch rival, C. R. Smith, invited him to a graduation at the American Airlines stewardess school. There, in the front row of graduates, in chic stewardess uniform, was Patty Patterson, about to begin her brief career as an American Airlines sky girl. Fortunately, by this time Patterson had become acclimated to surprises by his daughter; only a few weeks earlier, after being annoyed by a small plane that kept buzzing his home in the country outside Chicago, he recognized the pilot, Patty, who had been taking flying lessons unbeknownst to her father.

A Patterson obsession that endured through his airline career, is Safety, with a capital S. Safety was the first in his Rule of Five. For a non-flier and a non-engineer, he quickly developed an astonishing understanding of aeronautics. With a gift for simplification, he could reduce the technical lingo of this new and intricate science to terms anybody could understand. Soon after he replaced the 247s with Douglas DC-3s, Patterson began talking with Jack Herlihy, vice president in charge of operations, about a still better air transport plane. Herlihy, a Massachusetts Institute of Technology graduate who had started his flying career as a Navy pilot, had another MIT man, W. C. "Bill" Mentzer, as his assistant. Both Herlihy and Mentzer could translate laymen's dreams into engineering terms and vice versa. Both agreed with Patterson that what the airlines needed, for safety, speed, and profitable flying, was a four-engine airliner that would stay aloft on any two engines.

With this super-safe future airliner shaping up in his mind, Patterson called United's sales and operations people together in

1936. "What do we want in an airliner?" he asked them. Adopting the best of the ideas tossed at him, he had Herlihy and Mentzer draw up specifications for a four-engine luxury airliner that would carry up to 40 passengers, double the DC-3 load, at 230 miles per hour. Patterson laid this big idea in airliners before Frederick B. Rentschler, head of United Aircraft Company in Hartford. Rentschler called in his chief engineer, George J. Mead, and Commander Jerome C. Hunsaker, MIT's aeronautics wizard, to help on power and wing designs.

With these blueprints in his briefcase, Patterson called on his old cronies at Boeing Airplane Company. They were too busy engineering a four-engine flying boat, the Pan American Clipper, first plane to carry passengers across the Pacific and the Atlantic, to waste much time or effort on an airline man's airliner. So Patterson took his blueprints to the Douglas plant in Santa Monica, where canny Donald Douglas pointed out that building the first experimental model might cost as much as $600,000.

"Are you serious or just shopping around?" he asked Patterson.

"We'll underwrite half of the engineering cost, if you'll foot the rest of the bill," said Patterson. Douglas agreed.

This was the inception of the DC-4, in 1936, which Douglas thought he might be able to produce in quantity for around $200,000. Rival TWA's executives heard about the project and asked if they could join in. "Sure, come on in," agreed Patterson. Then Pan American, Eastern, and American joined in underwriting the venture, with Douglas still paying half of the development cost. United underwrote one-fifth, the rest was divided among the other partners. It was 1939 before the triple-tailed monster — for those days — rolled out of the Douglas plant. As the promoter of the ultimate in airliners, Patterson had first claim to two months of demonstration flights over the United system. When test pilot Benny Howard cut one engine as the airliner was roaring down the runway at Cheyenne Airport which is 6,200 feet in altitude, and the plane lifted smoothly into the rarefied air on the remaining three engines, Patterson beamed and Jack Herlihy exclaimed, "That's the plane for us!"

American Airlines' pilots had the next turn. TWA, meantime, had counted itself out by ordering five new Boeing-designed four-engine planes called Stratoliners. Boeing engineers had changed their minds about the future of land planes and their Stratoliner had a pressurized cabin enabling it to carry passengers at higher altitudes. Patterson never got to add the original DC-4 to the United fleet. Both United and American engineers suggested so many changes after the test flights of the X-model that Donald Douglas proposed selling it to the Japanese who were shopping for a long-range military transport. This relieved United and the other airlines of their underwriting obligations. Patterson's dream plane came to an ignominious end at the bottom of Tokyo Bay on a test flight.

Douglas promptly built an improved single-tail DC-4 but before deliveries could be made, Patterson was called to Washington by the War Department. The Army Air Force had decided that the DC-4 was just the airplane needed to transport top brass, troops, emergency supplies, and diplomats around the world fast in the looming global war. Patterson was asked to cancel United's order for a fleet of the luxury plane he had pushed to reality. Reluctantly, he did so. As the Army C-54 and the Navy R-5D, the DC-4 became the aerial workhorse of the war. United struggled along with its fleet of DC-3s. Not until 1945 was Patterson able to pick up some Army surplus DC-4s and remodel them for airline use. By then, they were outmoded by the larger, faster, pressurized Douglas DC-6, the Lockheed Constellation and the double-deck Boeing Stratocruiser. But the dream airliner had served its original purpose of bringing safety, comfort, and dependability — the first three of Patterson's Rule of Five — to air transport. And by this time, United's resourceful chief was thinking in terms of the jetliner revolution on the airlines.

Safety meant more than well built, dependable planes of course. The early thirties brought a revolution in the technique of flying transport planes. Pilots no longer flew by instinct and experience, pitting their wits against the elements and hurtling through space by sheer courage and luck. Marvelous new scientific gadgets were coming to their aid. It was a difficult transition for the old seat-of-the-pants fliers who trusted their reflexes more than the little black boxes and the wiggly lines on new scopes in their cockpits. Patterson became the champion of the new techniques for flying. Anytime a pilot or an engineer or anybody else had a great idea for making flying safer, Patterson was his backer against the doubters. Most of the other airline heads were veteran pilots, but it was non-pilot Patterson who bought and tried the innovations that the old-timers often considered impossible.

When Patterson moved his base of operations from Seattle to Chicago in 1931, he took along an eccentric friend and genius named Thorp Hiscock, another ex-banker who had married the sister of Bill Boeing's wife. Hiscock happened to be in Boeing's home one evening when the bad news arrived that a BAT plane had crashed east of the Rockies in a storm. Boeing lamented that everybody but the pilot knew about the furious storm front moving across the western prairies. Somehow he had missed the warning flares lighted at emergency landing fields along the airway.

"If we'd only had some way of talking with the pilot, this accident wouldn't have happened," said Boeing, adding that he had put the problem of two-way radio telephoning between the ground stations and planes in the air up to all of the big radio companies, only to be told that this was an impossibility.

"It's possible to build two-way radios for planes," declared Hiscock impetuously. "I can build one myself."

Within hours Hiscock was launched on the project. Knowing nothing about electronics, he tried every trick that only a rank amateur would think up. He finally managed to talk between his home in Yakima and automobiles winding over the Cascade Range, then between the ground and an airplane flying directly overhead. When Hiscock seemed lost in the electronic maze, Patterson hired an engineer from a radio laboratory to help him. The expert quit at the end of the first day, declaring, "That fellow is crazy." Patterson was inclined to agree one day when he picked up the phone in his office and heard "The Two Black Crows," a popular radio team, discussing the fuzz on peaches. He waited a while and lifted the receiver again. The Two Black Crows were still de-fuzzing peaches.

"What's going on here?" he asked his secretary.

"It's that nut, Mr. Hiscock," she explained. "He's playing records over the plant telephone exchange to make interference for his new plane-ground radio set."

Shortly, Hiscock brought Patterson a two-way, plane-ground radio set that worked — with a good many disconcerting squawks and squeals. Convinced by this crude model that talking with pilots in flight was possible, Patterson found the money to establish a radio laboratory at the Oakland, California, PAT terminal. Western Electric joined in the project, as did Herbert Hoover, Jr., who was working on the same problem for TWA. Before long, airline pilots no longer flew unwarned into wild storm fronts.

The radio problem solved, Hiscock became a roving researcher. With Patterson's blessing, he roamed the United air lanes seeking ways to take the guesswork out of flying. Patterson and Hiscock became fast friends. When Patterson moved to Chicago, Hiscock made Chicago his base too. Until their families could join them, the two men shared an apartment — with much loss of sleep for Patterson as he was obliged to listen to Hiscock's middle-of-the-night inspirations. Hiscock's most brilliant ideas usually hit him about three o'clock in the morning, when his voice came booming

Does "Profit" Have to Be a Dirty Word?

IN OUR COUNTRY—*the world's prime example of economic progress—there are those who regard profits with hostility. They seem to believe that normal healthy returns are rather sinful and that large returns are downright immoral. In their lexicon, as someone has said, profit is a dirty word. My question is, would we have a better air transportation system if there were no profits? Would it be better if the airlines made just a little profit, enough to keep them alive but feeble? Or is the industry entitled to a healthy profit that will permit it to pay good wages and ample dividends, to liquidate debts expeditiously and accumulate financial strength for further advances? Coast-to-coast air travel became possible in 1927 but it called for a strong back, an adventurous spirit, and $400 to pay the fare for a trip that took 32 hours—at least on paper— and there were no in-flight movies to pass the time. Today you can fly by jetliner from one coast to the other at a fare 63 percent lower than in 1927 and at a speed increase of over 500 percent. If the advance in safety, comfort, and other intangibles could be expressed mathematically it would exceed 500 percent. Now I ask, could this advance, unparalleled in the history of transportation or any other industry, have been made without profit? If "profit" is such a dirty word, why don't we talk about wages for stockholders just as we speak of wages for workers?*

W.A.P.

through the apartment, "Are you awake, Pat? Listen to this."

One night Hiscock had an inspiration for a device to regulate the temperature of fuel in flight, thereby increasing the efficiency of the airplane's engines.

"Sounds great, Thorp," agreed Patterson, sleepily. "Better go to work on it in the morning."

"Morning, hell. I'm going out to build one now," replied Hiscock, bounding out of bed. At the United shops he hounded mechanics for three days and nights, munching popcorn for nourishment. Before he left the shops he had proved up another scheme for making flying safer.

Another time, while he and Patterson were lunching at the Edgewater Beach Hotel, Hiscock became too absorbed to eat watching a frozen flag dangling from the mast of a nearby building. Every time a brisk wind whipped the flag it shook some ice loose.

"That's the answer," exploded Hiscock, abruptly leaving Patterson to finish his lunch alone.

During the next five days Hiscock evolved some long rubber tubes to attach to the front edges of the wings of planes. As the tubes were inflated and deflated by air pressure, the action whipped the ice off the wings. This first practical deicer for the wings of transport planes reduced the hazards of flying through chilling clouds and fogs and snowstorms. Another time he spotted at a machinery show a hydraulic device designed for earthmoving machines on the Boulder Dam construction job. He bought it and lugged it to the United shops where mechanics were working on an electric control to change the pitch of propellers after planes had made their altitude climb.

"Forget electricity," he told them. "Do the job with oil."

Though engineers and mechanics were skeptical, Hiscock pestered them until they tried out his idea. Before long, pilots on all airliners were changing propeller pitch hydraulically and flying more efficiently and safely at various altitudes.

When the man with the unquenchable curiosity collapsed and died prematurely in 1934, it was one of Patterson's poignant losses. At the time Hiscock was absorbed in a robot box that could keep an airliner on course while the pilot attended to other cockpit duties. A decade later, a robot became a reality.

"There'll never be another Thorp Hiscock," mourned Patterson.

With Hiscock's inspirations as a reminder, Patterson has always been ready to gamble dollars, millions of them if necessary, to back any reasonably feasible idea for taking the guesswork out of airliner operation. One that paid off was the hunch of Bert Ball, a United pilot and Boeing School of Aeronautics graduate with an absorbing interest in air mass meteorology. Ball's flight reports often included some gratuitous observations on storms he had encountered. Hearing about these, Patterson told United's operations heads:

"This fellow's on the trail of something. Let's let him have a plane for a while and see what he finds out."

Ball and a young radio technician rigged up a flying laboratory, gathered a hurry-up crew of five college professors and five radio technicians. Day after day, they flew into air mass fronts fresh out of the Alaska cradle of weather and bumped with them over the Oregon and California mountains until the storms petered out over the prairies. When they finished their rough skyriding, the flying researchers had proved that the static which raised havoc in the pilots' earphones was generated by the metal plane itself; also, that stubby cables attached to the trailing edges of wings would discharge the static without crackling into the earphones.

Another time, R. W. "Shorty" Schroeder, vice president for safety, was telling Patterson about the need for an instrument that would record weather and altitude at every mile of an airliner's flight, as a check on the pilot's reports. A few days later, Patterson mentioned the problem to a Baltimore instrument manufacturer.

"We've got a new portable recording gadget for testing the humidity control of air conditioning equipment," said the Baltimore man. "I bet it could be adapted to flight recording on airplanes."

"I'll have two technicians from our communications lab over at your factory by tomorrow morning," replied Patterson.

In a few days they converted the humidity tester to a barographic flight analyzer. There were two extra pens on the instrument. The technicians actuated these to record the periods when the pilot turned his controls over to the automatic pilot and also when he used the plane's radio transmitter. Patterson had a barographic flight analyzer installed on every United Mainliner. They turned up astonishing new data on how pilots were flying the airliners.

Patterson had been intrigued with ideas for dispelling fogs at airports, even temporarily, to bring airliners down more safely, and with radar "seeing eyes." When United's communications chief, Russ Cunningham, an old PAT pilot, and veteran meteorologist Henry Harrison, hit on a radar searchlight that could spot the furious cyclonic hearts in thunderheads, Patterson found $4 million — as much as the entire United fleet of 60 Boeing 247s cost in 1934 — to install a seeing eye in the nose of every Mainliner.

Another time Patterson was in a San Francisco hotel when one of his pilots called him from Oakland Airport.

"Pat, I've got it," he shouted. "Come on over, I want to show you that I've got it."

"Got what?" asked Patterson.

"Instrument approach. I can cut the runway every time."

Patterson hustled over to Oakland Airport. Ragnar Freng, a big, blond Norway-born pilot was waiting for him, with his five-year-old daughter. In his eagerness to demonstrate his new gadget, Freng had forgotten to take the little girl home. He put her on the floor of the warmed-up plane with some jacks to play with, pushed Patterson into the co-pilot's seat, taxied to the end of the runway and took off. After circling over San Francisco Bay, he adjusted some instruments, pulled a black hood over his head and let the little black box fly the plane to within 50 feet of the landing strip. Freng took off and landed 22 times to convince his boss that "blind" approaches through "the soup" were feasible and safe. The CAA didn't buy Freng's technique, nor did fellow pilots, but Patterson bought Freng.

It Takes Enthusiasm to Get Results

WHEN I FIRST BECAME *president I took a cold look at my job and concluded that I was merely the fellow who motivated ideas and policies, the success of which depended upon many people. I realized I couldn't get results without enthusiasm on the part of these people. If a man knows why you ask him to do something he can give you enthusiastic work that is reflected in the service you're selling. In the early days, we had no industrial relations experience. We had to get most of our ideas from our employees. I decided I would have to talk with them face-to-face and spent up to a third of my time out along the line listening at all hours of the day and night to the people who did the airline's work. I've listened to a lot of chatter but out of it has come an occasional gem. The result was better work and better service.*

W.A.P.

"How would you like to take over as supervisor of pilots?" he said.

"I don't know," replied Freng. "I don't know how the old-time pilots would like it."

Patterson persuaded him to take the job. It was the beginning of a period of change that separated the old-time, seat-of-the-pants fliers from the scientific instruments pilots. Freng started at the eastern end of the line and convinced most of United's pilots that the day of instinctive flying was past and the era of mechanical aids had come. Airliners were flown from the ground as much as from the air. For every pilot in the air, Patterson has pointed out repeatedly, United has 40 skilled technicians on the ground. During his years as head of United, Patterson has earmarked more than $100 million to test and prove up ideas for making airliner flying safer. He has insisted that any safety device developed by United pilots or technicians be made available to all competitors.

"Safety is not something to be patented for anybody's exclusive use," he holds. "The only person's life that I have any right to risk is my own."

CHAPTER V

The Personal Touch

When he was unexpectedly catapulted into the presidency of the reorganized United Air Lines Transport Corporation, 34-year-old Pat Patterson was the youngest and probably the greenest of the airline's top executives. Most of his associates were old-timers in their forties, with a decade of experience behind them in an infant industry for which no textbook had been written. By contrast, Patterson had only four years of experience as an air transport man, two in Seattle, two more in Chicago.

"When I took a cold look at my job," he has recalled, "I realized that I was merely the fellow who would be motivating ideas and policies, the success of which depended upon many people out on the line."

Patterson wanted to talk with the people out on the line face-to-face, to listen to their ideas. His ambitious goal was to see every person on the United payroll at least once a year. To him, employees were not merely a commodity to buy; they were partners, as interested as he was in making the airline run smoothly. Most of his key management people were experienced ex-pilots; he had never flown a plane. Several were engineers with degrees; he hadn't graduated from any college. His legal training was a smattering of night school business law courses. He had never sold a ticket or manned a passenger gate. But he had a sponge-like capacity for absorbing technical information and pigeonholing it neatly in his capacious memory. During his first year's talks out along the airway, he gleaned such a liberal education from fellow workers eager to tell him how to run an airline that he resolved to spend up to half of each year, if possible, visiting United's stations. His understanding wife estimates that this added up to the equivalent of almost three years of their early married life.

It was an unorthodox way to run an airline. Few company presidents could have stood up to these "talkathons," as they were nicknamed. But Patterson, still in his mid-thirties, was full of vim and vigor and zest. For him, the sessions with United people were the spark of life.

"Pat likes people — he loves to get the feeling of people first-hand," explained Harold Crary, who was United's first executive to open an office in Chicago.

Added Bob Johnson, another veteran vice president out of the Seattle incubator, "Pat always has had this ready sense of humor. He could give and take. His small stature was an advantage; he didn't dominate anybody. He was always one of the group — any group. He had a forceful personality. Everybody had a lot of respect for his integrity. He was young looking, but it was a young business and everybody was young."

"Pat never sat down at a desk," recalls Russ Ahrens, another Boeing Air Transport veteran who outranked Patterson in seniority by one year. "He'd sit on a bench or a box or on top of a desk to make a session as informal as possible. He had this wholesome way of disarming people and making them feel at ease. He could get acquainted faster than anybody I've known. He'd begin by asking where the other fellow came from and all about his family. The next time he came, he'd remember the answers — who had been sick or what youngster had broken an arm — and ask first off how he was doing now. He kept up this continuity of interest in everybody connected with the airline — pilots, dispatchers, mechanics, ramp workers, janitors, anybody."

Patterson made some surprising discoveries out on the line. In Boeing Air Transport shops, for example, he learned that it was the practice to fine workers for mistakes or for dropping parts and damaging them. The company had deducted some $47,000 from paychecks in fines. In North Platte, he met a butterfingered mechanic who had paid $1,400 in penalties. At Midway Airport in Chicago another mechanic told him, "I'm afraid to pick up anything." Back at his office, Patterson called in the airline's treasurer and asked him to make up a list of workers who had paid fines and how much they were. Then he dictated a letter saying he thought there must be a better way of getting rid of accidents, and ordered United's treasurer to send a check to each penalized worker returning his fine money. The mechanic in North Platte was overwhelmed with his $1,400 Christmas present. He quit dropping things and shop errors dropped all along the BAT routes.

To most of the 1,400 people out on the line, their inquisitive, youthful president was "Pat." It came naturally to call him by his first name rather than Mr. Patterson. His prodigious feat of remembering names, particularly first names, became legend. Patterson admits that he fudged a little on this. When he was alone, after a talkfest, he jotted down names and pertinent facts in a little black notebook, from which he dictated memos to himself when he returned to his office in Chicago. His secretary typed the notations on cards, which were bunched by areas served by the airline. The cards gave him a quick refresher on people when he revisited Spokane or Toledo or Fresno or any other station.

Before long these early jottings toted up to a handy record of families, personal problems, or potentials of United people. They were the one-man start of what became eventually the most sophisticated employee vital statistics record kept by any corporation. Many key United executives and supervisors owe their first promotions to the memos Patterson dictated about them in the thirties. These were the years when the employee roll was small enough for an indefatigable young chief executive to know everybody who worked for him.

They were rugged years financially. All of the airlines were scratching for passenger revenues, which frequently blew out the window following headlined airplane crashes. Patterson was not only meeting payrolls and buying planes. He was "squandering money," so some of his stockholders sometimes thought, on a medical blanket for United families, on a retirement pension plan, on a personnel department, on an employee credit union, and on training for United people ambitious to get ahead. In the struggling thirties, these somewhat intangible bonuses to employees were sometimes labelled "Patterson paternalism"; in later years, as the nation's social outlook matured, "Patterson paternalism" was reevaluated as the thinking of a young company builder who was two to three decades in advance of his time. Explains Patterson:

"I have always had a horrible distaste for paternalism. I have tried to be thoughtful and helpful and my rule has been to have our personnel people inquire if anyone in trouble needed and wanted help, and give it if they did. But I never wanted to become a mother hen to United employees."

In his huddles with employee groups, whether in a shop, a ticket office, or on the ramp, Patterson always started the give-and-take with inquiries about "your problems," then adroitly swung the conversation around to working conditions and possible "beefs," and wound up inviting tips on how to run United better. He gleaned many earfuls of gratuitous advice. Plenty of workers in Oakland or Elko or Des Moines or Newark knew just how they would run the airline if they were pushing the buttons on the president's desk in Chicago.

"Sure, I listened to some dewy ideas," recalls Patterson, "but I picked up plenty of practical suggestions, many of them innovations that have helped make United Air Lines what it is today."

One dilemma was how to keep the reservoir of ideas flowing when the inquiring president was somewhere else on the airline. Patterson hit on the answer during one of his early tours of California stations. He was talking with a radio man at San Francisco

Airport at three o'clock one morning when the operator remarked between messages, "Our whole communications system is loused up with messages involving getting a seat for somebody. There must be a better way of making reservations."

"Give the problem some thought and let me have your ideas," suggested Patterson.

The next day in Los Angeles, he heard the same complaint from the other side, from a young reservations agent. Again Patterson asked for ideas for improving the haphazard system.

"Can you wait a few minutes?" asked the agent. "I've got a plan to show you. It's at my home, only four blocks away."

Patterson had time to wait. The young man returned with a reservations plan for the entire United system all blueprinted. It made a lot of sense.

"How long have you been working on this?" asked Patterson.

"Almost a year."

"It looks like just what we need. Why didn't you submit it?"

"Well, I didn't know how to do it without causing friction or resentment."

"You're going to Chicago to set up this system," Patterson told him. "From now on it's your project for the company."

Stopping off in Cheyenne, he encountered a young mechanic with an idea for a better airline heater that had been peremptorily shelved by his supervisor. "Let's have another look at this," said Patterson. Before long, the better heater was in use not only in United Mainliners but in DC-3s of other airlines as well. The company and the inventor were sharing $15,000 a year in royalties.

"We've got to make it easier for people to make suggestions," Patterson told his executive staff on his return to Chicago. "Here's a reservoir of ideas we haven't tapped."

The result was the Suggestion Conference, established in the mid-thirties. Composed of six rank-and-file people and six supervisors, the conference met monthly to consider ideas submitted for operating any part of the airline more effectively or more economically. During the next two decades almost 200,000 suggestions poured in. Some were so simple that anybody could have thought of them — but hadn't. Ray Rieder's suggestion, for example: individual lockers for ground service personnel where soiled work uniforms could be left and fresh uniforms picked up, an idea that saved United $300,000 in a decade and won Rieder a $3,000 check at the end of the first year. More than 30,000 suggestions have been adopted, and their originators have been rewarded with checks ranging from a few dollars up to many thousands, depending upon how much the bright idea saved the airline. Over the years, the checks have totalled more than $1 million.

"These suggestions have saved United many millions," Patterson says, "But that's just the dollar side of it. The suggestion conference has been worth even more in morale. It keeps everybody on his toes, trying to run the airline better."

By the early forties, the personal touch approach had jelled into a practical and effective employee relations philosophy. But putting it into practice had become an exhausting undertaking, even for a vigorous young president with a built-in supercharger. Instead of 1,400 names to remember, there were now 4,500, and during the war years the United family exploded to 13,000, not counting 1,500 people temporarily absent in uniform. Like all airlines, United was virtually an arm of the military service and Patterson was obliged to spend much time in Washington, uncorking air transportation bottlenecks. With every seat on every flight allocated by government priority, there was no selling to do. Airline wage scales were frozen. Many good workers, particularly in sales and service, were quitting to earn more in booming war industries.

In a valiant effort to stem this tide, Patterson made one of his top business-getters, Russ F. Ahrens, his administrative assistant. Ahrens was a large, economy-size, alter ego for Patterson. Fresh out of the University of Washington, he had gone to work for Boeing Air Transport in San Francisco a year before Patterson joined Boeing in Seattle. His first assignment was pasting airmail stickers on every mailbox in San Francisco. Ahrens was just married and his proud young bride described him as "a junior executive with Boeing Air Transport." While still a banker, Patterson recalls meeting Ahrens one day on Market Street, "the only junior executive

Building Pride into Your Team

IT IS MY THEORY *that you should lay a brick a day to let your people know you are thinking about them. In building esprit de corps, it's not the big things but the thousands of little things that count. You have to make every one of your people feel he or she is an important part of the organization. I was in Seattle when one of our mechanics of Italian background told me, "My wife would like to cook you an Italian dinner." When I went out to their neat little home, their son insisted on taking me to his room. Hanging on the wall was a pair of miniature boxing gloves, with my card attached to them. I had sent them with a baby blanket to his mother a dozen years before when the boy was born. For over three decades I've sent flowers and get-well greetings to our people or anyone in their families who have been ill. If our medical people thought I should make a personal telephone call to someone who was ill, I've done it willingly. Whenever we receive a complimentary letter about an employee, we send him a copy for his scrapbook. We have an award system with "Oscars" in the form of a small gold airplane for outstanding service. We have other awards for outstanding civic service because the image of United Air Lines in our 112 communities is the reflection of the images of our people in those cities. One of our awards went to a man who organized a volunteer fire department, to another for helping his church, to still another for exceptional work with Boy Scouts—anything that creates a better image in the country.*

W.A.P.

I've ever known who carried a paste bucket." Ahrens recalls that first meeting and thinking that Patterson "looks like a kid," little realizing he was sizing up his future chief. Ahrens was born with Patterson's gift for meeting people easily. He knew from personal experience how Patterson felt about people: when his wife was about to give birth to their first child, Ahrens faced the problem of raising funds to pay for a serious emergency operation for her. He asked Patterson if the company would go on his note if he borrowed several hundred dollars from a bank.

"No," replied Patterson, "but the company will lend you the money interest free."

Ahrens' first assignment as administrative assistant was to re-evaluate the United sales people as quickly as possible and reassign them into more challenging jobs. He did this so well that Patterson made him vice president for personnel, to shake the personal touch gospel down into a technique that could be used by all of United's supervisors, as well as by the top executives.

"Russ, everybody working for United should be moving ahead, or should know the reason why," Patterson told Ahrens. "Everybody should be evaluated at least once a year and it should be the responsibility of his supervisor to give him an honest answer on whether he is going ahead or standing still or slipping backwards. Let's have the supervisor go over an evaluation sheet at least once each year with every employee. They'll both sign it, and if the employee doesn't agree with his supervisor's estimate, he can make a note of it and this will go into the record, too. The next year, they can talk it over again and see who was right."

This has been a fundamental principle of the company's employee relations ever since, as Ahrens built United's personnel department into one of the most advanced in the country.

When the war ended in 1945, Patterson was brooding over the turn of the wheel that had lost him his intimate touch with United's people. He had not been able to make any personal contact with some 8,000 of them, the new employees largely in the shops and on the ramps who had gone to work for the airline as wartime employees. He also felt a keen urge to renew touch with the 1,500 returnees from the armed services to whom he had guaranteed jobs when they doffed their uniforms. In one of his spontaneous inspirations, Patterson decided to organize a super talkfest covering the entire United system. It turned out to be the talkathon that ended talkathons.

Taking off from Chicago in a DC-3 converted to a combination flying office and sleeper, Patterson, Ahrens, and five other head office executives undertook to hit 36 United stations in 32 days. This was only the western leg of the proposed campaign. The group picked up regional supervisors as they flew west, south, and north. The talks with workers started with breakfasts and ended with dinners. They followed the old pattern — inquiries about families, answering questions, outlining plans for the future. It was a man-killing routine. When the party reached San Francisco, only two of the team that started on the expedition were on their feet. Patterson collapsed completely. At St. Mary's Hospital, doctors concluded after careful examination that he was suffering from total exhaustion. Five days in the hospital, followed by two weeks in a hotel, revived him, but he recalls that he "was tired for two years after that trip."

While he recuperated, Patterson had time to cogitate the well-meant crusade that had done him in. He concluded that meeting everybody on the airline face-to-face was no longer physically possible. His nimble mind hit on some less strenuous ways of maintaining the personal touch with more people. These techniques have worked and stood the test of time, as the United family exploded to over 40,000 men and women, scattered from Miami to Honolulu, from Boston to San Diego.

One innovation, now an institution, is the annual company awards dinner. These dinners don't catch everybody but they have enabled top executives, Patterson among them, to make a ceremony of employee recognition. They have been occasions for public recognition of exceptional service not only in the line of duty, but beyond the call of duty — work with Scout troops, Junior Achievement groups, churches, or other civic activities. The United "Oscars" are small gold airliners on pedestals and, for outstanding achievement, trips to Hawaii, all expenses paid, for employees and spouses. Beginning in 1956, they were topped each year by the "President's Award," a handsome gold plaque bearing a citation for the man or woman who had, in Patterson's opinion, contributed most that year to United's success and well being. The recipient of this highest of all company honors also received a handsome watch.

"What people crave most is recognition for exceptional work, particularly over and above what they are paid to do," reasoned Patterson. "United is a corporate citizen in every community it serves. The company's image is only as good as the employee who is serving his community."

Patterson is such a stout believer in public recognition of good work or exceptional service that he has made something of a fetish of parties for old-timers, such as the one in San Francisco for Bernice Johnson who early in 1966 celebrated her fortieth anniversary with the airline. She had joined Pacific Air Transport in 1926 and was the girl who rushed the Post Office checks for carrying the mail across the street to banker Patterson to cover Vern Gorst's payroll. Old-timers winged in from all over the United system to honor her.

Patterson and other top executives have thought nothing of flying from Chicago to Honolulu to whip up a dinner party for a service pin presentation to an outstanding employee. "It's a lot

more important to make a fuss over a one-year service pin than a five-year pin," says Patterson.

The company dinners that evolved out of Patterson's cogitations following his disastrous final talkathon almost always wound up with a free-for-all in which he or some other top executive fielded questions from the floor about the company and its policies. Patterson's explanation for this somewhat incongruous conclusion to a gala anniversary party is typical of his thinking.

"Any United employee is entitled to an honest answer to any question that any shareholder might ask at a stockholders' meeting," he says. "The shareholder invests his dollars. The employee invests his time and energy. They are equal partners. Sometimes they are one and the same, because a lot of our employees are stockholders."

Even with these company dinners, Patterson had an uneasy feeling that there were unasked questions in the minds of United people that should be answered. A good many employees, being on duty, could not attend the dinners. Some of those who did attend were too shy to ask questions in public. His solution for this gap was a new feature in the *UAL News,* later re-named *The Shield,* entitled "Your Visit with the President." In "Your Visit," he answered each month up to 30 questions mailed in by employees. Patterson made it clear that these questions were strictly confidential between him and the writer, even though he answered them in public. The questioner's name was never revealed, even to the supervisor to whom he might turn for information before replying to the question.

The questions have been fair and honest and to the point, as a rule. Over the years Patterson has answered about 5,000 of them. Now and then he found a letter from a ruffled employee who must have been thinking, "Here's one I bet the old man won't answer." But Patterson did dictate an answer, sometimes mailing it to the writer directly if the topic were too personal or controversial instead of printing it in *The Shield.* For Patterson, the day each month — usually a Sunday — that he devoted to answering letters was like old times out on the line. He invariably worked himself into the mood for swapping ideas with fellow workers, then switched on his dictating machine.

"Your Visit with the President" became *The Shield's* most popular department, always rating in reader polls far above other features. But it has been much debated among executives of the company. Some department heads feel that employees should talk with them rather than go over their heads to the president. Other executives feel just as strongly that open discussion of employees' grievances clears the air. Patterson believes that direct contact with workers makes them feel that the top echelon cares what they think.

Out of the early face-to-face contacts with United people have grown some other unusual company institutions. One is the vital statistics report, popularly known as "The Grapevine." It sprouted out of Patterson's habit of jotting down facts about the people with whom he had talked — items about accidents, illnesses, anniversaries, births, deaths. Wanting to keep posted between visits about events important to United families — graduations, weddings, scholastic awards — he urged supervisors to update him with memos about the workers under their direction. This grew first into small trickles, then streams, and finally torrents of vital facts, which the Personnel Department organized in a card index. From these grapevine reports, Personnel made up a larger report once a week, and sometimes more often, for Patterson's desk. Scanning it, he could tell at a glance which United families were troubled, or were celebrating, or had passed an important anniversary. Often on impulse he reached to the telephone and made a long distance call, on the theory that anyone out on the line enduring misfortune might be cheered by hearing from somebody up topside. When a veteran pilot lost two fingers working with a power saw, Patterson called his wife to relay the message that if the accident interfered with his flying, United would have another job for the pilot as soon as he recovered. An injured stewardess too speechless to talk when Patterson called her long distance made up for her lack of words later by telling everybody about her call from the president.

More often, Patterson clicked on his machine and dictated a letter, often accompanying it with a telegraphed order for flowers for a sick wife or the mother of a new baby. To babies, he dispatched small yellow blankets, with little dolls for the new-born girls and miniature boxing gloves for the mewling boys. When one worker wrote in to ask "Why didn't my wife get a baby blanket?" Patterson knew that he had hit on a potent employee relations device. He wrote to apologize for the grapevine's breakdown and dispatched a blanket. Thousands of appreciative letters have poured into his office. Typical was one received from a captain:

"At the birth of our daughter, over 20 years ago, the first gift we received was a blanket from you. After her passing recently, the first flowers were from you. The thing that makes this airline great is not the number of jets, the route miles flown or the money we make; its greatness is in the heart and the compassion of the people who run it."

These personal contacts with United's people triggered another kind of grapevine as important as the one that fed facts about people into Patterson's office. This reverse grapevine spread the word through the rank-and-file, as well as among supervisors, that United Air Lines was a company with a heart. It was an idea that Patterson worked indefatigably to make true.

"I keep asking myself, 'What kind of a person is United Air Lines?'" he said thoughtfully. "Anyone who devotes the best years of his life to United should be assured repeatedly that next to his family the company is his best friend in time of need. This airline is people as well as planes and routes. With most people it is the human and personal touch that counts."

In the course of his talks with workers, Patterson inevitably stumbled into reports of United people who were hard pressed financially because of illnesses or accidents or other misfortunes. In the early days he often loaned them money out of the company's treasury to tide them over the humps. His colleagues in the United financial department took a dim view of these impulsive loans by a supposedly hard-headed banker.

"These people might have fallen into the hands of loan sharks," he said. "We ought to have a way to lend them money at moderate rates."

Before long he found the way. It was the United Employees' Credit Union, launched with deposits by Patterson and other officers and by rank-and-file workers as well. Managed by a Board of Directors elected from its employee members (and permitted by United to carry out their duties on company time), the Credit Union has grown into an extremely healthy savings-loan concern paying worthwhile dividends to its members. It thus encourages them to save while, at the same time, providing a low cost loan source for those in need of financial help.

The Patterson formula for running the airline has always been a paradoxical blend of hard-headedness and sentimentality. To him, United Air Lines has always been a corporate person. When an executive objected to his policy of finding jobs for widows of former employees, he asked. "Would you want me to forget your wife under similar circumstances?" Back in the thirties, when so many United employees were in their early forties, he began worrying about their welfare two decades ahead when they reached their sixties. This concern for workers' senior years jelled into the first airline employee retirement program, launched in 1941. By the time he retired in 1966, the company had poured millions of dollars into the retirement reserves, even more than employees themselves had contributed. The unions had nothing to do with the program; Patterson dreamed it into reality long before union leaders were thinking in terms of pension fringe benefits.

During his trips over the line in the mid-thirties, Patterson began to have serious doubts about the value of the periodic check-ups of airline pilots required by the U. S. Department of Commerce. Prior to 1938 the physicals were given by local doctors who took their little black bags to pilots' hotels or homes and gave them perfunctory check-ups.

"I watched a doctor put a stethoscope on a pilot's chest and thump him, then take his blood pressure and poke a stick in his mouth and have him say, 'Ah,' and that was it," complained Patterson. "Maybe he was in good shape to be flying a plane and maybe he wasn't."

At the time, few physicians knew very much about aviation

Competition Is the Life of Trade

Sometimes I get *mad at our competitors for the silly things they do, and they get mad at us for some of the things that we do. One man's idea is another man's challenge to compete. Air transportation wouldn't be where it is today if it hadn't been for some rugged individuals fighting for business, each in his own way.*

W.A.P.

Human Relations

Human relations *come from the heart. My criticism of much of the effort being made by business to improve the relationship between management and employees has been the tendency toward a dependence on plans and mechanical procedures and devices to accomplish the objective. No plan of human relations is genuine unless it comes from the heart. Specific programs are only a means of executing a philosophy.*

W.A.P.

medicine. In 1937, Patterson heard of a young Army doctor at the Dayton Army Air Base who had specialized in the aero-medical field and tried to hire him to watch over the health of United's pilots. The young doctor was unwilling to abandon his Army career, but he promised to pass the word along that Patterson was looking for an aviation physician. A short time later a call came through from Colonel A. D. Tuttle, commandant of the Army's School of Aviation Medicine at San Antonio, Texas. Shortly, the peppery little colonel, who was about Patterson's stature, bounced into the latter's office. His enthusiasm for finding out more about the effects of high altitude not only on pilots but on passengers was contagious. Almost before he knew it, Colonel Tuttle was on United's payroll, with an appropriation adequate to set up the first airline medical clinic in the company's headquarters building across the street from Chicago's Midway Airport. Tuttle quickly installed X-ray machines and other impressive equipment designed to tell him in short order all about the physical and emotional condition of the men who flew the planes. As might be expected, his activities were viewed with alarm at first by the flying crews who feared that Colonel Tuttle's medical gadgets might ground them. But the pilots changed their viewpoint when they discovered that the Colonel was trying to keep them from being grounded by heading off disabilities.

The pilots' early grumbling was picked up by a few profit-minded stockholders, one of whom came to Chicago to voice his protest. Patterson took him on a personal tour of the gleaming new clinic. After sizing up the expensive looking equipment, the stockholder said, "This looks like a waste of the company's money to me."

Patterson pointed out a window at a new DC-3 that had just been delivered.

"Look at that wonderful machine," he said. "Look at those powerful engines in the wings."

The visitor agreed that the DC-3 was a fine airplane.

"Well, that wonderful flying machine is worthless until you put two minds in the cockpit," Patterson pointed out. "Those engines are no good to us unless we overhaul them every six months. Maybe they don't need overhauling that often, but we do it for safety's sake, and to be sure they don't wear out. Now — doesn't it make sense to overhaul the men who fly that plane every six months? This medical clinic we are in costs about the price of two DC-3 engines. Instead of a waste of money, I consider it a blue chip investment."

The stockholder raised no more objections. Neither did the pilots, as the first United clinic gradually grew into a chain of eight in major United centers from New York to San Francisco, staffed by 14 full-time doctors. In fact, the Air Line Pilots' Association adopted a resolution urging all airlines to establish preventive medical departments like United's. The doctors were all aviation medicine specialists, although they often spent more time on non-fliers than on pilots. In 1939, Patterson increased the medical budget to enable Colonel Tuttle's staff to check the company's ground workers, as time permitted. In similar fashion, an accident-sickness insurance plan was instituted to help relieve the bugaboo of sudden, unplanned medical and hospital expenses.

Rather than a medical program aimed at helping people who were already sick or injured, the United Medical Department has focused on preventing disabilities. Dr. George J. Kidera, the energetic young Chicago physician who worked with Colonel Tuttle and who succeeded him as United's Medical Director in 1949, took to the company magazine, *The Shield,* with a monthly question-and-answer column to alert United families on how to combat epidemics and common illnesses.

"It has paid off to keep our people fit," insists Patterson. "We needed a broad program of preventive medicine for everybody. One of the things I expect from our medical department is a sound heartbeat for the company."

Other airlines have sent their doctors to study the United Medical Department, which became the model for the air transport industry. In 1966, Patterson was voted the Airline Medical Directors Association Award for outstanding contribution to aviation medicine — the first time the honor was bestowed upon a lay person by the 4,000 doctors and airline scientists in the association. But long before that, he had had his reward for his foresight in pioneering United's unique medical setup.

The reward, in this instance, was his right leg. In 1950, he was afflicted with a painful blockage of a major artery in his right leg. A fellow director on the board of an insurance company persuaded him to go to a special clinic for treatment. There, after he failed to respond to treatment and blood poisoning was imminent, surgeons decided that the only way to save his life was to amputate the leg. A devotee of the active and strenuous life, Patterson rebelled, despite the intense pain the blocked artery was giving him.

"Nobody's going to think about amputating my leg unless George Kidera says it's the only thing to do," he insisted.

Dr. Kidera arrived and hustled the patient out of the clinic and into Chicago's Presbyterian-St. Luke's Hospital. There Dr. Ormand Julian saved Patterson's leg with a transplanted artery. The unusual operation was highly successful. Since then the artery has been replaced by a Teflon by-pass that has enabled Patterson to resume all of his outdoor activities but horseback riding.

A riding enthusiast, Patterson owned a handsome Arabian horse named Mr. Gallagher. A short time after Dr. Kidera had ordered him to give up riding Mr. Gallagher because the saddle pressed on the "Teflon leg," as Patterson calls his right limb, the doctor was called to the presidential office.

"George, I'm worried about you," began Patterson. "You have no hobby but hospitals. I want you to take up horseback riding. I'm giving you an Arabian horse to start with."

The Arabian horse was Mr. Gallagher, whom Dr. Kidera's small daughter Tina promptly renamed "Mr. Pat." Dr. Kidera took up horseback riding for two years. By that time Mr. Pat had to be put out to pasture with an ailment the veterinarian described as a clogged artery.

"The only difference," explains Dr. Kidera, "is that it was Mr. Pat's left hind leg and in Mr. Patterson's case it was his right rear leg."

Patterson likes to cite how the United medical plan unex-

Which Came First, Capital or Labor?

I HAVE A PHILOSOPHY *of business and an attitude toward personnel. I don't claim that my ideas are original, nor do I claim that they are orthodox. I think we are wrong in accepting the economic theory that labor is a product of capital. In my opinion you can argue just as strongly that capital is a product of labor. Efforts and ingenuity created capital at some time during the chain of events which has formed our economic system. I think they are so interwoven and so interdependent that you cannot refer to one without referring to the other. One group is investing capital and the other is investing time and effort. We used to refer to capital, labor, and consumers, but today we're practically talking about the same thing. Our 24,000 stockholders are not only capitalists but many of them are employees and many more are consumers. So how can you separate capital and labor and the consumer any longer? Today we are a part of a social and economic system. While we are producing for our own partnership of stockholders and employees, we must make a real contribution to the advancement and preservation of the system which we in this country enjoy. We are a small part of a tremendously big thing.*

W.A.P.

pectedly came to his aid when the hospital and doctor bills totaling $10,000 came in. The medical umbrella he had set up two decades before for the United family took care of 80 percent of the expenses.

"Suppose it had been a janitor in San Francisco instead of the president in Chicago who needed that Teflon leg!" exclaimed Patterson. Until his retirement, Patterson kept the Medical Department tightly under his own wing to be sure that no economy-minded budget committee ever shortchanged it. "Why look at the cost when it is one of our best investments?" he asked.

His sojourns in Presbyterian-St. Luke's Hospital pointed up the Patterson genius for leaving an impact on people. He was on first-name terms with patients, nurses, therapists, internists, everybody who worked on his floor. When Dr. Kidera came out of the room, everybody asked, "How's Pat today?" When Patterson was in the recovery room, following an operation, a seven-year-old boy lay on the next bed, tightly holding a little toy airplane with a broken wheel. Patterson noticed the broken wheel. The next day the youngster had a United DC-7 model to play with.

"He's the best patient in the world when he's sick, but the worst patient when he's well," was the way Dr. Kidera summed up Patterson, who had a new hobby, reading popular magazine medical articles. Kidera was obliged to read all of them, too, because Patterson was sure to ask, "Isn't this something that would help

Joe Smith?" or some other United employee whom the grapevine had reported as ill or hospitalized.

One day in 1952, Patterson commented to personnel vice president Ahrens that many of the faces he saw in the busy United Chicago terminal had been there for a long time.

"I'll bet a lot of these people are coming to work day after day with dreams of doing something different," he said.

Ahrens pointed out that the Chicago workers had been screened when they were hired and that they were re-checked each year by their supervisor in line with Patterson's decree that everybody working for the airline should be moving ahead or know the reason why.

"That's not what I mean," said Patterson. "I'm thinking about each man's or each woman's secret ambition. Maybe some of them would like to be president. I'd like to know. Maybe we're overlooking something."

Patterson and Ahrens decided to have competent interviewers talk confidentially with 1,800 employees. The result was an eye-opener. About 65 percent of the interviewees were well satisfied with their jobs; they wanted mainly to be left alone. Another 15 percent had what Patterson calls "ideas of grandeur," without the willingness or ability to improve their qualifications for better jobs. Twenty percent not only wanted to do something bigger and better, but they had the industry and willingness to qualify for better jobs. Many were studying at night school. The survey did turn up a young engineer frankly shooting for the presidency.

"That fellow needs broader experience," said Patterson. "Let's put him in economic controls, analyzing what's wrong with the company."

Patterson felt that he had hit "a great reservoir of talent" in the 20 percent of the company's workers with ambitions to get ahead and the industry to improve themselves. He immediately increased the budget for training promising workers for better jobs. The company was already spending many millions training flight crews. Before long it was spending as much on ground workers. By the time of his retirement this United "university of the air" had a budget that would run a good-sized college, about $20 million a year, roughly half of it for training people on the ground for better jobs. Scores of top supervisory people have been sent back to college, with full pay, for special training at Harvard, Stanford, the University of California, or the University of Chicago. Others who have resumed university studies on their own have had their expenses reimbursed when they completed their studies with satisfactory grades. To find these ambitious workers when the better jobs opened up, Patterson had the Personnel Department devise in Chicago a cross-indexed, automated file of talent and skills that he calls his "employee inventory."

"They press some buttons and out pop the cards of the people who can handle the job," he exults. "Twenty percent of 37,000 people gives you a lot of talent in a lot of fields."

A long list of United executives owe their positions to the uncanny Patterson sixth sense for seeing potentials in people. An enduring Patterson tenet is, "Promote from within." Only rarely has he gone outside United's ranks to find an executive. These were invariably professionals that even he could not dig out of the airline's rank-and-file gold mine.

As might be expected, Patterson's zealous interest in the personal welfare of the United family occasionally encountered rough flying. Some of United's executives have felt that his personal touch cuts through the line of authority. Now and then an employee has resented it, contending that his private life is his own affair and not the company's concern. The most vociferous opposition came from union leaders who argued that looking after workers was the union's and not the company's business. Patterson's reply is that the nine unions that have organized large segments of United's employees, from senior pilots to ramp workers and mechanics, have their roles in the airline business, but not to the exclusion of the company. Whenever the unions have negotiated a wage increase, he has immediately had the unorganized employees' jobs re-evaluated and, if justified, they got a corresponding raise. Patterson has been on first-name terms with union chiefs and has been a frequent speaker at union conclaves. But he has fought "featherbedding"

Labor
Is People,
Not a
Commodity

IN DEALING WITH *employees there is one economic theory I threw to the winds 35 years ago—the theory that labor is a commodity. Employees are human beings and cannot be treated as a commodity. My basic philosophy is that capital cannot be put to useful accomplishment unless there are human beings to execute the basic idea for which that capital was provided. I also believe that employees cannot be gainfully occupied without capital. Therefore we have an inseparable partnership. I accepted many years ago the fact that a human being, responsive to human treatment, deserved an amortization at least equal to that of an inanimate machine which we protected and amortized. We don't throw a machine into the scrap heap when it goes temporarily out of service due to a mechanical breakdown—and I don't think human beings should be thrown out under similar circumstances.*

W.A.P.

adamantly, even taking costly strikes rather than agree to pay for no work or make-work. During one strike, when pickets were marching outside his office, he paid $1 million in wages to 9,000 other workers caught by the strike, rather than have them undergo hardship, and called it another of his "good investments."

"I sincerely believe that true collective bargaining is sound and constructive," he concedes. "When all the ideas are contributed from one side, it is impossible for an employer to know if he is doing everything he can for his people. Unions call attention to things you wouldn't notice. But the employee showing enterprise, initiative and ability shouldn't be held down to the level of union contracts. If he's worth more, he should get more."

CHAPTER VI

Wings for Mars

One of the unique components in the Patterson structure has been his ability to see his pride and joy and at times his colossal headache, United Air Lines, through two pairs of eyes. One set is warm, bright, sparkling, bubbling with contagious enthusiasm. This is the set of eyes through which Patterson usually sees the airline. But every so often he turns on the other pair and appraises his masterwork, and himself, through cool and objective eyes, as he thinks rivals or passengers or federal authorities see United. This pragmatic Patterson took over in 1941 before the United States became involved in World War II.

Just prior to Pearl Harbor, Patterson flew to Washington, D. C. at the urgent behest of Edgar S. Gorrell, president of the Air Transport Association, to meet with other airline heads. Gorrell's political radar had picked up an alarming blip: in the event the United States entered the war, President Roosevelt intended to take over all airlines and operate them as an arm of the government, just as the railroads had been seized in World War I. Patterson and the other airline presidents could foresee that if this were done it might be catastrophic. They might never again be able to disassemble the federal air octopus; air transport could become a permanent government monopoly, as it was and still is in most countries. The presidents burned the midnight lights perfecting a plan for pooling their 363 airliners — of which 69 were United's fleet of DC-3s — their flying crews, technical staffs, shops, and know-how, to offer the military services a ready-made global air transportation system able to start flying overnight.

It was a lucky piece of foresight. After the Pearl Harbor attack, the President called Gorrell to the White House. General H. H. Arnold, chief of the Army Air Force, was already there. F.D.R. read an executive order he had just signed authorizing seizure of the country's airlines for the duration of the war and placing them under Arnold's command. The word had already leaked out. In the *Chicago Tribune* of May 15, Patterson read the dread headline, "Air Lines Go Under U. S. Rule." Nevertheless, Gorrell protested the wisdom of the drastic order and outlined the airline presidents' plan for operating their fleets as a private enterprise arm of the military forces. As a clincher he pointed out that, whereas the President's plan would take weeks to organize, the airlines could start flying Army and Navy personnel and strategic weapons that very day under their own proposal.

The President turned to "Hap" Arnold and asked him which air transport setup he preferred. To Roosevelt's surprise, Arnold made a convincing plea for leaving the airlines in the hands of the operators who had built them up and who knew from experience how to run them efficiently. Arnold, who had gained a year's headstart in aviation preparedness by persuading airplane builders to spend millions on warplane design before Congress got around to appropriating a single dollar, plunked squarely for contracting with the airlines for sky transport and for use of their shops for hurry-up modification of war planes. Impressed, the President tore up his executive order.

This decision probably saved the airlines again for private

enterprise. It also probably cost Patterson a general's star for his collar, because the President had planned to draft the top echelon of the airlines into uniform overnight. Later, Patterson was invited to attend the Army Command School at Fort Leavenworth for a concentrated course in war strategy. He finished the five-week course as president of his class and was offered a commission as colonel, which he declined. In a talk he was invited to make at the windup of the course, he declared:

"I never realized before the indebtedness we owe to the men who have elected military careers for their lives. I am going home with one idea — the magnitude of war."

He had already put his airline on a wartime basis. Every decision he made hinged on patriotic motives, regardless of the cost to the United Air Lines treasury. Soon after receiving word of the White House decision that kept the airlines intact, he called his regional managers together. The Air Force and the Navy needed carrier planes immediately, without waiting for new transport wings to roll out of aircraft factories which were jammed with fighter and bomber production. The only source was the airlines' fleets. The question was, how many of their 363 planes could the airlines give up and still operate as airlines.

"We have 69 planes," Patterson told the managers. "I want you to take off your United Air Lines hats and look at our needs and the country's just as though you were strangers and tell me how many planes we can give up and still continue to fly our routes."

After they had agreed upon a figure, Patterson jotted it down in his notebook. Then he went to Washington, where the War Priorities Board had put up a chart in a room in the Department of Commerce. The chart indicated how many planes the Military Air Transport expected each airline to surrender. It was the starting point for negotiations between the Military Air Transport Service and each airline. Patterson checked the figure in his notebook with United's expected contribution. The figures were almost identical. United was to give up 36 planes, leaving 33 of its DC-3s to maintain service.

"Gentlemen, I can settle United's part in this deal in ten minutes," said Patterson. "What you want from United is perfectly all right with me. We'll deliver the planes to you as you need them."

In the ensuing weeks, Patterson found that his remaining 33 planes had to carry more traffic than the 69 had handled prior to war's outbreak. Passengers on official business, many of whom had never flown before, jammed ticket offices. They and military personnel in a hurry to get to new posts pushed the regular customers out of the airliners' seats. Patterson laid down the rule that military and government personnel came first, civilians next, which meant last and often not at all. The DC-3s, which had been flying 60 percent full before the war, now took off with every seat occupied. They averaged 11.4 hours in the air each day, over two hours more than in pre-war days. Two "milk runs" from the east coast to the west coast, carrying ferry pilots back to airplane factories in the Pacific Northwest and in Southern California, were sold out solid every night far ahead. Loyal passengers who had flown United during the rugged thirties were vociferous in their wrath at being pushed back on the already crowded trains. United was definitely in their doghouse. Patterson hustled off to Washington with a plan to lift the onus from the airlines. He urged a government-run priority agency, with offices in key cities, to decide who should get the all too scarce seats on the airliners.

The War Priorities Board did in fact adopt a plan which divided prospective air passengers on a priority basis. Holders of Number 1 priorities, on vitally important war business, could bump Number 2 priorities off the airliners any time and any place. Number 2s could bump Number 3s, and the 3s could bump the 4s. The system failed to make "the hopers," clustered around the embarking gates, any happier but at least it assured seats to VIPs who were on important government missions. From Patterson's staff, the War Priorities Board drafted traffic manager Ray W. Ireland to head the government's travel priority mechanism. As a new Army colonel, Ireland had to reverse his technique; instead of luring passengers aboard the DC-3s, he now specialized in saying "No."

Despite the loss of half of its fleet, United was flying with handsome profits. The thought of making money from the war when hundreds of United's pre-war staffers, ultimately 1,500 workers, were making the sacrifices required of men and women in uniform, caused Patterson much loss of sleep. Early in 1942, he hit on a device for taking at least some of the airline's profit out of war. This was a non-profit, wholly-owned subsidiary, called the Victory Corporation. "Victory" would handle all contract flying, the training of technicians, pilots, and mechanics in United's school, and all modification work done for the Air Force in United's shops. It was a great and patriotic idea, but short-lived. The war procurement agencies in Washington balked at making unorthodox non-profit contracts with United, and orthodox cost-plus contracts with other airlines. After a few months of tilting with bureaucratic windmills, Patterson had to let the Victory Corporation die a premature death. In its place, he set up another device: scrupulous audits of costs for services rendered the war agencies.

For a former banker supposedly hardheaded about nailing agreements down in writing, Patterson had a disarming disregard for formalities when it came to war services. When the Air Force wanted a "milk run" launched from its Dayton, Ohio, supply base across Canada to Alaska's Aleutian outposts, he dispatched planes and crews without waiting for papers to be signed. Two weeks later, the Japanese were invading the Aleutians. The 2 million miles of Alaska flying in all kinds of weather and over all kinds of terrain was a valuable training course for United crews when they were assigned in September, 1942 to "Operations Pacific." This was an oceanic airline launched in 42 days to supply American troops in their island-hopping from Australia to Japan. As boss of Operations Pacific, Patterson reached into his already skeletonized staff of key executives for Seely Hall, a veteran Oregonian who had joined Vern Gorst's pioneer airline even before Patterson had taken Pacific Air Transport under his financial wing. Hall's orders from the military were often so top secret that not even Patterson or any other United executive knew where Ops Pacific's 25 crews were flying. Sometimes, Hall himself didn't know, unless he happened to be aboard a plane that took off from San Francisco with sealed orders to deliver men or materials to the other end of an 8,600-mile airline whose westernmost terminal might change en route, depending upon which islands were being hopped.

Ops Pacific caught Patterson in a difficult bind. Top brass ruled United's civilian pilots could not be paid more than Army or Navy pilots who were under the military umbrella. United's pilots thought they ought to have at least their regular pay for the hazardous transpacific flying. So did Patterson. He reported to the Secretary of War that he could not sign a contract that chipped away at his pilots' paychecks. The War Department withdrew the proposed Ops Pacific contract. Nevertheless, a call came through from an Air Force general in Dayton saying that an airborne troop needed a load of parachutes for an island invasion in the South Pacific, and needed them in a hurry.

"Well, General, where are the parachutes?" asked Patterson. "We'll fly them out today and talk about contracts tomorrow."

All of the 2 million miles of Alaska flying and much of the early transpacific carrying by United crews was done before a scrap of paper was signed. While flying Ops Pacific sans contract, Patterson evolved a pay arrangement acceptable to the pilots. Always an unabashed fliers buff, Patterson's eyes sparkle as he recalls the flying feats of United crews who winged over Japanese island bastions to search out narrow metal landing strips hastily rolled out in jungle

clearings. He delights in pointing out that many of United's top pilots graduated from these wartime crews, trained for oceanic flying at United's school in Oakland, California. Ops Pacific also proved a training ground for some key executives. Engineer and pilot W. E. Rhoades was one. As first officer to Captain Ralph Johnson, Rhoades flew the first American 1,960-mile, nonstop Perth-to-Brisbane flight across Australia with a load of military people.

Later "Dusty" Rhoades, a captain in his own right by this time, flew the C-54 transport "Philbert II" on a 31,380-mile globe-girdling flight that touched 40 countries, carrying military and state department advisers from Washington, D. C. to Cairo for a Roosevelt-Churchill-Chiang Kai-shek conference, thence back to San Francisco via India, Australia, and Hawaii. One of Rhoades' passengers was General MacArthur's chief of staff, Major General R. K. Sutherland, a veteran flier who occasionally spelled Rhoades in the pilot's seat. Shortly, "Dusty" Rhoades was in a colonel's uniform as pilot of "The Bataan," the famous plane in which Mac-Arthur made good his laconic "I shall return" to the Philippines and in which the General flew unarmed into Tokyo on V-J Day.

Scarcely a month after he had saved the airlines from government seizure, General "Hap" Arnold had Patterson on the phone. The general had some bombers to be remodelled for a special mission. Could United's overhaul base at Cheyenne, Wyoming, handle the job? Sure it could, Patterson assured him. Shortly, two Flying Fortresses touched down at Cheyenne airport. Under direction of Air Force technicians, United mechanics removed bomb bays and guns, replaced them with photo equipment and installed extra gas tanks wherever they could be hooked up. These first two bombers were followed by 5,734 additional aircraft remodelled by United at Cheyenne. The overhaul base, augmented by two huge new modification hangars hurriedly erected, surrounded by a trailer and tent boom town, mushroomed into the country's largest and the model for several in which other airlines made over bombers fresh out of aircraft plants. General Arnold found it more expeditious to keep the bombers rolling off the assembly lines and install the newer improvements at the modification centers than to change production lines in the factories.

As more transport planes came out of the factories, the Air Force returned some of United's commandeered airliners. The DC-3s were filled to capacity. It was an airline man's dream, more passengers than he could handle with no selling effort necessary. Instead of being delighted with the happy situation forced upon him, Patterson worried. He could see the hard-hitting sales force built up during the lean years disintegrating. Patterson had the money to pay people more, but orders from the War Stabilization Board prevented him from rewarding employees in pace with the rising cost of living. He tried an end run by talking the WPB into allowing payment of a 5 percent cost-of-living bonus to United's workers. The WPB order excluded anyone earning $10,000 a year or more. Patterson stormed down to Washington to plead for more money for the executive group. Though he managed to get the ceiling raised to $12,000, this left out the airline's top echelon people, including the president himself. Patterson attempted to offset the salary freeze with public recognition for outstanding service. Typical was an open letter in 1942 to Seely Hall, the peripatetic boss of Ops Pacific, reading:

"The 15-year service badge which you and 60 of your fellow employees are wearing symbolizes the greatest asset our company possesses — the experienced, competent, loyal people who make up our organization. We can buy airplanes and gasoline and hangars, but we cannot buy experience, and experience is that invaluable element which gives an organization its character and personality.

"We are a young organization, and we are especially proud of you and your associates who are holders of two-diamond service pins. This is why we are publishing the enclosed advertisement in *American Aviation, Western Flying* and *U. S. Services* for August. (signed), W. A. Patterson". The pat on the back didn't take the place of a fatter paycheck but at least it let everybody know that the boss appreciated their work.

In the hectic war years, the personal, human touch that Patterson had worked so hard to achieve was slipping. The brooding president felt that it had to be revived somehow. One device was to enlarge the staff of carefully chosen information girls in key United centers whose duty was to report to the president's office whenever the family of any employee on leave in the armed services needed help. These "first aid" girls helped find homes for families, they lined up sitters for working wives, they checked families with illnesses. Patterson's office and Personnel under Russ Ahrens followed up with messages of cheer and flowers for hospitalized wives, and blankets for newborn babies. Even in the hectic war years, the personal touch came shining through.

At war's end, after 37 million miles of military flying including 7,000 Pacific crossings, and after modification of 5,736 aircraft at Cheyenne, government auditors showed up to check and renegotiate United's pay for war services. Patterson was ready for them. United's accountants had already gone over all costs for war work with sharp pencils.

"We've already audited our books and we think we should reimburse the government $296,000," he told the surprised government accountants. "I'm going to give you a check right now."

This refund proved to be just about the exact sum the federal auditors arrived at after carefully checking the cost sheets for war services rendered, both with and without contract.

Instead of easing the pressures on Patterson, the war's end intensified them. Thousands of pre-war passengers who had been bumped from airliners for the duration wanted their seats back. More thousands who had become air-travel minded wanted these same seats. Airports became bedlam, both inside and out. Above them, in bad weather, arriving airliners were stacked in layers 1,000 feet apart waiting to be talked down to landing strips. Inside, travelers with pockets full of money crowded the lobbies and scrambled for reservations. Too few planes attempted to accommodate too many passengers. United had recovered most of its lost DC-3s, but the more sophisticated passengers wanted to fly in the four-engine airliners that had been girdling the globe as military carriers. Even so, the DC-4, which Patterson had imagineered in the thirties and pushed to reality only to lose it to the Army and Navy, was already obsolete. Every night the Navy was flying a souped-up DC-4, known as "the Hotshot," nonstop coast to coast. Although no airline could afford this luxury service, it was a portent of what was to come and what the air traveling public wanted.

The aircraft factories were not building more DC-4 vintage airplanes. They had better airliners in the works, larger, more powerful, pressurized planes that could fly higher and faster. None of these were available immediately. But the War Surplus Administration had military DC-4s to burn — or at least to unload at bargain prices. Reluctantly, as a stopgap, Patterson bought a fleet of these and had them remodelled into fairly plushy, albeit slow Mainliners, the modifications costing more than the planes themselves.

The bargain-price war surplus planes quickly created a new dilemma for the harassed airlines. Military pilots, out of uniform and looking for new livelihoods, spotted an opportunity to crash into the glamorous air transport business. With shoestring backing, scores of "non-skeds" sprang up. They carried passengers at fares approximately half those established by the CAB for the scheduled airlines. The non-skeds had little of the overhead of the scheduled airlines, they were not bound by the same safety regulations, they could shift routes from the northern sky paths in summer to the south in winter, skimming cream off the traffic of established airlines. This, too, added to the chaos on the airways.

When
We Need
a Friend

I HAVE A VERY *strong feeling based on some experiences in life that if a company is worth being associated with, it must demonstrate its real interest in its people at a time when the chips appear to be down. This is when true friendship and interest is of real value. One of the most pleasant experiences I have had throughout the years is the satisfaction of being able to assist my associates and, above all, it gives one such pleasure to observe that all of the supervisors in the company seem to have that same genuine interest that I feel must be sincere.*

W. A. P.

United met the post-war crisis with typically Patterson thinking and years-ahead planning. The first move was to earmark over $1 million to intensive company training courses. The objective was to rebuild the tight esprit de corps of the United team when the airline swung into war service in 1941. Three out of four employees who had joined United during the war had missed this training. The 1,500 returnees from military service needed it, too. "We've got to spend money making our people as well as our planes better," Patterson insisted. This was a long-pull program that would pay off in the years to come.

Meantime, the immediate problem was to get the airline back in efficient operation without delay. Gathering United's top executives into his office, Patterson detached three vice presidents from their desks in the new headquarters building across the street from noisy, busy Midway Airport in Chicago. The threesome, Ray Ireland, Hal Nourse, and Russ Ahrens, soon nicknamed "the atomic committee," was detailed to spend weeks or months, if necessary, out on the line solving problems on the spot. Patterson delegated authority to this committee to overhaul procedures, change schedules, buy ground equipment, hire or fire or do anything else to step up efficiency right now. The committee's whirlwind tour was drastic medicine that relieved pains, but it failed to heal the wounds of war.

Even before the war was over, Patterson had found himself in a lively crossfire on the international scene. Most of the larger domestic airlines had flown overseas military routes for the Army or the Navy, though none (with the possible exception of Pan American Airways, not a domestic carrier) had racked up the mileage or the number of flights scored by United's pilots. Nearly all of these operators had roseate dreams of winning for peacetime flight the profitable long-haul routes they had learned at government expense to fly. Quite naturally, Pan American, the giant U. S. international operator excluded by the CAB from domestic routes, opposed allowing the domestic airlines to invade the overseas field. Astute Juan Trippe, founder and head of Pan American, could see only hard times ahead on the international routes if several privately owned American airlines cut into the Pan Am melon, battling for traffic not only with each other but also with a score of state-owned foreign airlines.

Quite unexpectedly, Trippe discovered he had an ally among the domestic operators. In a speech at Chicago's Edgewater Beach Hotel in 1943, Patterson urged federal legislation to bar all domestic airlines from transoceanic flying. For this outspoken position, Patterson was panned in editorials in newspapers from New York to Santa Barbara as "an opponent to free enterprise in aviation." He was in a difficult spot. That same year, at the invitation of the Mexican government, he had gone to Mexico City to make a personal survey of Lineas Aereas Mineras, S. A., a struggling airline that needed help. LAMSA had been launched on a shoestring by a venturesome American pilot, Gordon S. Berry, primarily to fly valuable minerals from remote interior mines and to carry supplies to these mines. It had grown haphazardly to a 1,700-mile airline stretching from Mexico City to Nogales and Juarez on the U. S. border. In 1943, LAMSA needed a shot of vitamins, in the form of Yankee dollars, to keep it alive so that it could bring out much needed minerals.

Intrigued, Patterson loaned $250,000, with the option to buy three-fourths of LAMSA's shares, if the CAB approved. The CAB did approve, as did the Mexican government. Patterson sent a number of United executives under the leadership of Allan Bonnalie to Mexico City to help run the airline. United's flow of dollars in LAMSA grew to $5 million. In a speech in British Columbia in 1945, Patterson told of plans for United-LAMSA flights from Vancouver to Mexico City. But the Mexican and United States governments never seemed to be able to button up the bilateral air treaty that would have enabled him to hook up LAMSA and United at San Diego or some other border point. Patterson finally unloaded his south-of-the-border subsidiary to a group of Mexican financiers. Eventually, rival Western Air Lines bagged the Los Angeles-Mexico City route previously flown only by Pan Am.

The frustrating LAMSA experience firmed up Patterson's conviction that the U. S. domestic airlines should stay within the country's boundaries, or function through a "chosen instrument." This would be a cartel in which each domestic airline might have an investment but leave the flying to Pan Am, which unquestionably had the most know-how in overseas operating. All of the home airlines could feed traffic to the chosen instrument and share in its earnings. The chosen instrument would be one big and strong U. S. airline that could compete on even terms with government-owned foreign airlines.

When Juan Trippe publicly proposed the cartel scheme at the end of the war, an outraged cry of "monopoly" greeted the idea. The heads of 15 domestic airlines drew up a declaration demanding that the CAB deny approval of it. When Patterson was asked to sign this anti-monopoly declaration, he refused. Like the other presidents, he had been eyeing prospective overseas routes, particularly to Alaska and Japan where United pilots had millions of miles of flying experience. But the surveys of Hal Nourse and his statistical wizards had convinced him that, based on pre-war travel figures, the overseas bonanza was a rainbow. There just wouldn't be enough passengers to fill the airliners of several competing American lines and those of eight to a dozen foreign governments. When Patterson publicly backed Trippe's "chosen instrument" idea, he immediately became a pariah among the country's domestic airline presidents.

"Airplanes have demonstrated their ability to fly virtually anywhere and everywhere," he said. "No place will be more than 60 hours distant from any other spot on the earth's surface. But our studies have shown that, even in the Number 1 North Atlantic area, for the next five years, there will be less than 1,000 first-class passengers per day. This traffic could be handled by 43 airplanes each capable of carrying 100 passengers. If the United States and seven foreign competitors share the traffic, it means six airplanes for each country. If all of the U. S. airlines were granted equal rights in the transocean carrying, along with all the government-owned foreign lines, we might have as many as 22 companies competing to do a job that would require only 43 airplanes. That is why United Air Lines takes the stand that one or more chosen instruments

Informed Employees Are Better Employees

I HAVE BEEN WORKING *since I was 14 years of age. I have worked hard and have been well treated by my bosses. I never forget that, for it is the basis of my philosophy of management-employee relations. When our company was smaller, I managed to talk with every employee at least once a year. When this became impossible because of the number of United employees, I met with larger groups in the major centers along our system. I wanted to get their viewpoint firsthand and to answer their questions firsthand. I believe that every employee is entitled to a candid answer to any question he wants to ask me about our business. The secret is to be completely honest and candid. I have enjoyed these contacts with our rank and file. I would not want to take my immediate subordinates' word for what people on the ramp are thinking. For the past 15 years I have devoted a day a month to answering thoughtful questions in our company magazine. I get myself into the mood of those early day visits with employees out along the United system and then dictate my answers as though I were talking personally with a pilot, a mechanic, a ramp worker, or a reservations agent in one of our ticket offices. I think an employee is as entitled to ask questions of management as the stockholder who puts his money into the company. The employee puts himself into the company.*

W.A.P.

should represent this country, under private enterprise, in coping with the competition of government-owned foreign monopolies in the international flying field."

The "chosen instrument" idea proved to be a temporary tempest. The CAB never approved it. Patterson delights in recalling how, a few weeks after he was being denounced as "Juan Trippe's stooge," he was battling Pan Am for routes to Alaska and Hawaii. The CAB denied United the route to Alaska, but granted flights to Hawaii first from San Francisco, later from Los Angeles. Soon, "Stooge" Patterson was spearheading the domestic airlines' fight to keep Juan Trippe's planes from flying Pan Am's overseas passengers across the United States, proving that air transport politics make changing bedfellows.

Slowly but steadily, the airlines pulled themselves out of the post-war chaos. Patterson was again able to focus on building an airline dedicated to his gospel, the "Rule of Five." United Air Lines, which had detoured into war service as a big little business, was now a full-scale big business with a future as unlimited as the skies above.

CHAPTER VII

The Swift Magic Carpet

For most of his business life, Pat Patterson has been on the lookout for a better airplane, the right airliner for the right flight. He began his presidency with a fleet of wrong airplanes, foisted on the airline by the plane and engine builders who had formerly owned United Air Lines. Though the 247s were the first modern airliners — a Boeing engineer, admiringly looking at one at the 1933 Chicago World's Fair predicted, "It will be a long time before anyone builds a better or faster plane than this" — they had already been outmoded by a better and faster plane in the making at that very moment. Stuck with 60 of the 247s, Patterson was finally forced to switch to DC-3s.

Since that lesson in 1934, it has been a basic part of his philosophy that airliners should be "imagineered" by the airline people who have to operate them. Plane builders didn't think so back in 1934. Patterson's one serious quarrel with Phil Johnson, the man who put him into the flying machine business, was over this belief. "You'd better stick to flying the planes, Pat, and we'll design and build them," Johnson said, when Patterson brought the specifications for his first dream plane, the DC-4, to the Boeing Airplane Company plant in Seattle. No longer tied to Boeing, Patterson hunted a plane builder who was willing to let airline operators specify the airplane they thought they needed. Since then, he always has had a better plane in his hat, or else being blueprinted by United engineers.

Patterson's three-decade safari for the right plane has brought out some intriguing highlights in his character. To his way of thinking, the first requisite of an airliner is maximum safety. After that comes dependability and passenger comfort. Finally, the right plane has to turn in a profit for the airline. But Patterson has unhesitatingly invested millions in airliners that he suspected would not be money-makers to make sure passengers had the utmost in safety and comfort, or to keep pace with competitors in speed and dependability. Another Patterson maxim is that a more expensive airplane is often the best bargain in the long run.

The day of the multi-million-dollar magic carpet that could whisk travelers from Chicago to New York or San Francisco or Denver with the plushy comforts of crack trains began in 1947, the year the DC-6s joined the United fleet. Over the years Patterson had been asking passengers, "What do you want in an airplane?" Most of them didn't know. Those were the days when air travelers regarded themselves as adventurers. They uncomplainingly put up with bouncing through clouds, queasy midriffs, the din of noisy fuselages, ear-popping on landing, the squeeze of tight-fitting seats, wobbly legs on disembarking. They even took in stride the lukewarm meals, the delays to change spark plugs. Flying was the daring and romantic way to travel. Air passengers enjoyed bragging about their rough and thrilling flights.

Patterson sensed that his passengers would not buy this romance forever. And there were many thousands of potential passengers yet to make their first flight who had to be lured somehow into airliner seats. Ever since becoming an airline man, Patterson had thought of airplanes in terms of people, the crews who flew them, the passengers who rode in them. Most airline operators in the pioneering days were satisfied with military planes modified and adapted for passenger carrying. Patterson wasn't.

The DC-6, basically an enlarged, more powerful, pressurized DC-4, revolutionized air travel in many ways. The Sixes carried up to 64 people with new comfort and an atmosphere of hospitality. Air travelers discovered the enjoyment of pressurized cabins. At 18,000 to 20,000 foot elevation, they were as easeful as on terra firma. Meals, served from newly designed galleys, were an appetizing treat. Ears ceased to pop. Air sickness practically vanished thanks to efficient new ventilation systems that changed the air inside the plane every ten minutes. Engine din no longer drowned out conversation. Pilots had time to tour the cabins and greet passengers. Stewardesses called passengers by name. The hours aboard a DC-6 measured up to Patterson's theme that "people aboard our planes are guests in our home."

In the cold thin atmosphere outside their cozy cabins, the Sixes brought about innovations even more revolutionary. Flying three miles high they no longer had to follow the historic buffalo trails and stagecoach and rail routes through mountain passes that pioneer airline pilots had followed. The Sixes winged high above the tallest mountain peaks on flight paths often hundreds of miles wide of the early airways radio beams. Sophisticated new radar equipment enabled pilots to improvise flight paths that detoured storm fronts and headwinds. Often a dogleg flight much longer than the shortest route brought the airliner homing into its destination in shorter time and with fuel to spare, thanks to the push of tailwinds. It looked as though the golden age of air travel had arrived.

But Patterson's crystal ball, his intuition, fortified by the charts of statistical wizard Hal E. Nourse, whose studies took much of the guesswork out of tomorrow in the airline business, told him otherwise. Though the DC-6 turned in handsome earnings for United, it was already outmoded. Most serious limitation was its range, 3,600 miles. The DC-6 could fly nonstop across the country in favorable weather, but it lacked sufficient reserve for safety if the terminal airport was socked in and the airliner had to seek an alternative haven.

Patterson's radar also sensed that the era of the propeller-driven plane was about to end. Neither he nor United's engineers could say when the jet age would come. But jet military planes had swept prop-fighters out of the sky in the closing years of the war, and it was just a question of time until the new jet engines would do the same to propellers on the airways. After listening to a talk in 1947 by Air Commodore Frank Whittle, British inventor of the jet turbine engine, Patterson braced Jack Herlihy, head of United's engineering staff.

"Whittle's claims for the jet engine are fantastic," he exclaimed. "If what he says is so, the jet era is almost here."

Herlihy agreed. "It's just around the corner," he said.

"Well, I'd like to see United the best-informed airline on jets," replied Patterson. "Why don't you set up a group to find out all there is to know about them?"

Herlihy promptly put together the jet committee, headed by engineer Ray Kelly. The committee not only studied jet turbines; it had pilots boning up on how jetliners would fit into the traffic patterns designed for propeller planes. A number of senior pilots were sent to Air Force training centers for firsthand experience in flying military jet planes. At the time, the uncertainty that worried airline operators was how the 600-mile-per-hour jetliners might mesh into 300-mile-per-hour propeller-plane traffic without collisions. To find out, the jet committee operated a "paper jet airline" for one year. Each day, simulated jetliners took off from San Francisco and New York on imaginary flights to see how they meshed into flight movements around airports. Other airline operators viewed this game with amusement, particularly when Herlihy announced one day, "We cracked up a paper jet over Des Moines." But the paper jet game satisfied United's operations people that jetliners and propliners could fly the same airway safely. After the United paper jet findings were made available to airplane builders, Donald Douglas told Patterson, "It is amazing how much we got out of that study."

In 1950, Patterson dispatched Herlihy and Kelly to England

to fly the British turbo-jet Comet, already in production and available. They returned enthusiastic about the smooth flight of the Comet, but reported it too small and too short in range for United's routes. The jet committee went back to work on their own specifications for the ideal jetliner. Patterson brought United's operations and service people into the act. Since the jetliners would carry twice as many people as the DC-6s, he had a mock-up of the fuselage of the proposed jetliner built at the San Francisco maintenance base. Seats and galleys were installed. Groups of prospective passengers were invited to enjoy jetliner meals and service without leaving the ground. These experiments worked the kinks out of taking care of a hundred or more passengers in each airliner. United engineers, collaborating with Douglas Aircraft designers, evolved a strictly passenger jetliner. Unfortunately, jetliners on paper carried no travelers to their destinations and passengers were clamoring for faster transportation right away.

"How long will it be before we have jetliners in operation?" Patterson asked Herlihy in 1947.

Herlihy decided to play it safe. "Nine to ten years."

"Well, we can't wait that long. We've got to have some long-range planes before that," said Patterson.

United had just been granted a certificate to fly between California and Hawaii. During the war United pilots had made more than 7,000 flights over the route in the military version of the DC-4. To lure passengers off luxury ocean liners and into the sky, Patterson wanted to make the California-Hawaii flights the most deluxe air travel offered by any airline anywhere. The Boeing Airplane Company had designed the Stratocruiser, a pressurized, double-deck airliner with a downstairs salon where passengers could relax when they wanted to stretch their legs. The Stratocruiser was a commodious long-range land plane shaped something like the squat seaplanes Boeing had built for Pan Am's pioneer ocean flights. Patterson persuaded United's directors to authorize the purchase of a dozen Stratocruisers. They provided a ten-hour sky journey at its luxurious best, with champagne, wines, meals served in courses, and a native Hawaiian steward to help the stewardesses extend the aloha. Air travelers never had it so good, nor have they had it so good since.

The Stratocruisers were a high in air travel luxury but they turned out to be an economic headache. With their blunt noses pushing the air instead of splitting it, they were under-powered and their engines had to roar at full throttle. Expensive to fly and to maintain, they couldn't garner a dollar of profit for United's treasury. One day Patterson was talking with financial vice president Curtis Barkes about the costly flying elephants. The British Overseas Airways Corporation had grounded their Comets, the world's first jetliners, after two Comets had mysteriously exploded high on the skyway to Africa.

"I'll bet BOAC could use some long-range airplanes in a hurry," he commented. "See if they'd like to buy our Stratocruisers."

Barkes contacted BOAC executives. They were interested, but short of cash. "Sell them on any terms," advised Patterson. Shortly, the Stratocruisers winged off for London. Eventually they earned enough for their new owners to reimburse United for their original cost. Patterson switched to DC-6s temporarily for the Honolulu run. United began to make money flying over the Pacific.

But only temporarily. A new money-losing luxury airliner joined the United fleet in 1954. This was the DC-7, a longer-range more powerful version of the DC-6, which the Douglas Aircraft Company had somewhat reluctantly evolved two years before at the insistence of C. R. Smith, Patterson's perennial sparring partner and president of American Airlines. Smith wanted the DC-7 to compete on equal terms with TWA's Super-Constellation in non-stop transcontinental flights. American's DC-7s and TWA's Super-Connies were pulling the transcontinental travelers off United's DC-6s, which had to refuel at Chicago. Despite misgivings about the DC-7s' potential as money-makers, Patterson recommended to United's directors that they authorize purchase of 25 of the DC-7s. When they did, he told them, with a twinkle:

"Gentlemen, you have just bought $45 million worth of obsolete airplanes."

Our Basic Responsibility

To GET DOWN TO *basic philosophy: if you were to ask 100 executive officers, "What is your basic responsibility and what is your basic interest?" it is my guess—confirmed by conversations I have had with other chief executives—that 50 percent would reply, "My basic responsibility is to the stockholder, the owner of the company." The customer would probably be ranked second and the employee third. When anyone asks me what I consider my first responsibility to be and to whom, I say the public, the customer. And if I am asked to name the second, I say the employee. And then, third, the stockholder. In that order. Now let us see how logical that is. Without the customer you would not be in business. And without the employee to execute the great plans you have, some good, some bad, the plans might as well never be made. In the final analysis, this philosophy benefits the stockholder. Some years back I was invited within a period of one month to join the boards of directors of two large insurance companies. To help decide which invitation to accept, I asked the president of each company where he placed his basic responsibility. One president said his basic duty was to his stockholders. The other replied that his first duty was to his policy holders. I joined the board of the latter company and have never regretted the decision.*

W.A.P.

But the "obsolete" DC-7s provided United passengers with much pleasurable travel. To dramatize the new luxury service, Patterson loaded the first DC-7 delivered to United with a party of press, radio, and TV notables for a dawn-to-dusk flight from New York to Honolulu — breakfast in Gotham, dinner at the Royal Hawaiian Hotel on Waikiki Beach, with one stop in San Francisco.

The 70-passenger airliners, priced at $1,800,000 apiece, were an expensive but necessary interim airliner until the paper jet could become a reality. Soon after ordering the DC-7s in 1952, Patterson again asked jet expert Herlihy for a forecast.

"How long before we will be flying jetliners?" he asked.

This time, Herlihy was more specific in his prediction. "Seven years," he replied. Herlihy missed the target date by only four months.

"We can't wait that long," said Patterson. "We need more long-range planes now."

With no other better airliner available, the directors appropriated $60 million to buy 33 more DC-7s, bringing the United long-range fleet up to 58. Time proved this reluctant decision to be a wise one. By 1955, when the first prototype jetliner built in the United States was in the air, the DC-7s were carrying the bulk of United's burgeoning traffic load.

The first jetliner to take to the sky wasn't the custom-built job that the United jet experts had evolved in close collaboration with the Douglas Aircraft designers. Boeing's president William M. Allen, in a daring move, had invested $16 million of the company's money to develop a 100-passenger jetliner from a jet tanker the company had been building for the Air Force. The swept-wing Boeing 707 was flying before Douglas designers had finished their drawings for the proposed DC-8 jetliner. Patterson and his staffers had flown in the 707 and liked it, except for one feature. The fuselage was too narrow for passenger comfort, particularly for six-abreast coach seating.

One of Patterson's long-time phobias has been "sardine loading" of passengers in tight-fitting seats and still narrower aisles. Pan Am had just plunged on an order of 707s for overseas traffic. Patterson wanted to be the first domestic airline operator to go jet. The cost was tremendous, $6 million per jetliner.

"The first airline to order a jetliner fleet will either revolutionize the industry or go broke," he declared. "This time we've got to be right."

In a mood to invest $175 million, more than he had paid for all of United's 160 propeller-driven Mainliners, Patterson and the company's jet experts flew to Seattle for a final session with the Boeing top echelon. The 707 wasn't exactly the gleam Patterson had had in his eye since 1947, but it was a close facsimile thereof. By surprising coincidence, the 707, an outgrowth of a military plane, and the DC-8, with strictly commercial airline specifications, were almost identical in size, speed, range, and carrying capacity. But the 707's cabin was too narrow, by United calculations.

"Can you change the cabin's dimensions and make it two feet wider?" asked Patterson.

Bill Allen bounced the question to his chief engineer, Wellwood Beall.

"We can make the cabin longer, but not wider," replied Beall, with finality.

"Well, we'll have to go down to Santa Monica and see what Douglas can do," said Patterson.

The next day at Santa Monica, Douglas engineers agreed to build the DC-8 jetliner with a wider fuselage. But the DC-8 delivery date was more than a year after that of the 707. Patterson decided to wait for the right plane, even though American Airlines and TWA might fly rings around United temporarily on the transcontinental runs. In what he has characterized as "the most important decision in United Air Lines history" Patterson signed the $175 million contract with Donald Douglas for 30 DC-8s on October 25, 1955.

The order was the kickoff for the jet age on the country's airways. Within a fortnight, American, TWA, and several other airlines had contracted for fleets of 707s — with fuselages the Boeing engineers suddenly found they could enlarge after all, after losing the United order to Douglas.

American and TWA launched 5½-hour transcontinental jet service between California and New York in the fall of 1958. For almost a year, Patterson had to watch former United passengers stream through rival airlines' gates to board the 707s. United's slower DC-7s flew almost empty. To cut costs, Patterson discontinued coast-to-coast flights between California and New York and diverted the DC-7s to runs which had no jet service. Flying more economically at reduced speeds, and with seats filled, they made money. United's jetless first year of the jet age showed a handsome profit, instead of the anticipated losses.

On the morning of September 18, 1959, Mrs. Vera Patterson snipped a rope of carnations at San Francisco Airport and passengers boarded United's DC-8 Flight 800 for New York. The jetliner completed the 2,286-mile flight in 5 hours, 18 minutes. DC-8 Flight 801 brought the first load of jet passengers from New York to San Francisco. Early in 1960, Patterson celebrated the airline's takeoff into the jet age with a DC-8-to-the-50th-State "dawn-to-brunch" jetliner flight from New York to Honolulu, with the same group of press, radio, and TV notables that had been his guests on the DC-7 dawn-to-dusk flight in 1954. Westbound, the jetliner was "The Queen of the Skies." Sometime during the three-day Hawaii layover the name on the nose of the DC-8 was changed to "Annie Johnson." The winged "Annie Johnson" bettered the sugar schooner *Annie Johnson's* 1913 sailing voyage of 23 days to San Francisco considerably, and Patterson felt no twinge of either seasickness or airsickness. But he and his guests shivered when they disembarked in aloha shirts in eight-below-zero weather in Chicago. The jetliner "Annie Johnson" had overflown San Francisco to ride a jetstream wind nonstop from Honolulu to Chicago in 7 hours, 52 minutes. This was the forerunner of many fantastic speed records, as the jetliners shrank the globe. It also dramatized another Patterson foible. He likes to think of geography in terms of hours and minutes instead of miles. To most people, the United States is 2,286 miles from coast to coast; to Patterson it is 5 hours, 18 minutes wide.

The jet age quickly catapulted Patterson into a spree of high finance that would have staggered his old Wells Fargo chief, President Lipman. A single jetliner cost as much as the entire fleet of 60 Boeing 247s owned by United when Patterson became president. But a single jetliner earned dollars faster than 60 of the 247s. Like most airline presidents, Patterson had an idea that the company's slower propeller-driven planes, retired from the longer flights, could amortize themselves on shorter runs or by carrying cargo. Nobody could have been more wrong. After sampling jetliner speed and comfort, air travelers quickly developed an allergy for noisy prop-powered planes. Jet turbines might scream in the ears of people on the ground at take-off, but they were quiet to passengers in the cabins. Gone was the vibration and the din that once fatigued air travelers. Patterson's quick intuitive sense told him that the entire airline had to swing as rapidly as possible to an all-jet fleet.

"We can't afford to be half-jet, half-propeller," he concluded, after studying cost and earning reports of the jetliners. "Even freight goes cheaper by jet." He ordered three DC-8 freightliners from Douglas.

This was a timely discovery. He was negotiating for a fleet of Lockheed Electra turbo-prop planes for United's shorter runs. Herlihy and other United engineers were dubious about the turbo-

props. Patterson himself thought passengers might have misgivings about looking out cabin windows at whirling propellers instead of the motionless jet pods on all-jet planes.

"Let's wait this one out, until we find the right airplane," he decided.

Sud Aviation of France had designed a revolutionary new airliner, known as the Caravelle, powered by two jet engines in the tail. This gave the passengers a quiet ride, but United's engineers questioned certain technical aspects of the airplane. In the meantime, however, highly favorable reports from a passenger standpoint were filtering in to Patterson who then decided that a closer look at the Caravelle was in order. Consequently, in late November of 1959 in discussions with J. A. Herlihy and W. C. Mentzer, Patterson suggested that they take a couple of pilots over to France and fly the airplane with the reminder that, "maybe it's just what we want."

The group went over to Europe as doubters but came back so enthusiastic about the Caravelle that Patterson ordered 20 of them. When the French jetliners began flying United's eastern flights in 1961, air travelers were equally ecstatic about them. Unfortunately, the Caravelles were sweet-flying airliners but not sweet-flying money-makers after Patterson cut their seating capacity from 84 passengers to 64 in line with his crusade for greater safety and comfort. But their purchase was another piece of Patterson luck; within a short time the Electras, which he almost bought and which competitors did put into service, were ordered by the FAA to fly at reduced speeds until unexpected "bugs" could be worked out.

The airline's need for a larger jet for long intermediate flights, such as Chicago-San Francisco or Seattle-Los Angeles, was more difficult to solve. No airplane builder had just the right jetliner, one that would fly as fast as the big DC-8 or the 707 but carry less weight in engines and fuel. Patterson came near adding the Convair 880 to the United fleet, but turned it down because the cabin was too tight. Then Boeing designers scaled down the 707, knocking off 50,000 pounds of weight, and came up with the 720. This met United's need. The 720s joined the United fleet in 1960.

Our Obligation When Accidents Occur

DURING THE PAST *three decades I have made it my business to go to the scene of more than 70 percent of our accidents. Not that I've been eager or willing to do it, but I wanted to share the burden of the loss to the families of the victims. I have forced myself to go—to look and listen and do what I could to soften the impact of the loss, both to the families of passengers and the families of our crews. I would not trade that experience for anything. It is one thing to hear reports of an accident at your desk but if you want to know the full impact of such disasters, you have to go and see for yourself. Not enough responsible people do that. I have attended investigations of accidents since the early days of our airline and many times I have walked out of the room thinking, "That accident did not happen last night; that accident started the day that man went through our employment office. We should have found out then that he did not have the right qualities." We might have found out, too, that he was just the right man for some other duty on the airline.*

W.A.P.

Patterson wanted still another jetliner, a smaller one with wide cabin, for the shorter intermediate routes, one that would fly as "la belle Caravelle" flew but carry twice the load, 100 passengers or more. Boeing engineers explained that the jetliner Patterson wanted was an impossibility with available jet engines which turned up one-fourth more power than was required for short intermediate flights.

"Why not leave one engine off?" he asked.

The Boeing engineers had not designed a three-engine plane since they came out with the tri-motored 80-A in 1928, the year before Patterson became a flying machine man. With some doubts they went to work on a stubbier 720 with three engines in the tail area. The resulting 727 exceeded their expectations and Patterson's too. It was a jetliner with a cabin as wide as the 720's but shorter, and flight characteristics that were right for 300-to-500 mile hops. Patterson ordered 40 of them to start. Placed in service early in 1964, the 727 Jet Mainliners quickly became the most popular jetliner flying, both with the passengers who rode in them and the pilots who flew them.

Even with four types of jetliners, Patterson was still looking for an airplane to make the United fleet all-jet as quickly as possible. This was to be a little jet, for the short hops handled by Convairs, DC-3s, and later by Viscounts inherited from Capital Airlines. Three airplane builders had focused on this short-range jet field. The British had the BAC-111, already in production. Douglas had the DC-9, almost ready for delivery. Boeing had taken a design originated by United's Bill Mentzer and "Dusty" Rhoades, and engineered an airliner to be known as the 737. Whether or not Boeing would build the 737 depended upon a United order. It was a two-engine jet, with engines in the wings, a six-abreast fuselage, the same configuration and atmosphere as in the 720s and the 727s. Douglas had put the DC-9's engines in the tail, and the fuselage allowed for five-abreast seating only. The BAC-111 was eliminated from the contest because economic studies indicated it to be too small for profitable operation on United's routes. The contest narrowed down to the Douglas DC-9, already in production, and the

Boeing 737, for which United would have to wait a year while rivals were flying DC-9s on the now highly competitive short runs. The United sales staff wanted the DC-9 to meet the competition right away. The engineering staff still held out for the 737, mainly on the grounds that it was the more efficient airplane, with seats and other accessories interchangeable with United's 720s and 727s.

"Well, we've waited twice before for the right plane and never suffered," said Patterson. "I guess we can do it again."

He put the decision up to the directors. They listened to the sales staff spokesmen, then to the engineers. Meantime, President Bill Allen of Boeing offered to lease a fleet of 727s to United to bridge the time gap until the 737s could be delivered. The directors decided to go along with Patterson and the engineers. It was the largest commercial airplane buy on record, including 70 of the 737s; 20 standard 727s plus 15 new 727 QCs, designed for quick conversion from passenger to all-cargo service; and seven 200-passenger Super DC-8s. This $750 million order concluded Patterson's three-decade safari for the right airliner for the right route. The blueprint for United's switchover from the propeller era to the all-jet age was completed.

If Patterson has been daring and bullish in his enthusiasm for jetliners, he has been just the opposite in his attitude toward the SSTs, the supersonic airliners of tomorrow — meaning the 1970s — that became the big airlines' major dilemma in the early sixties. Recognizing that the day of the supersonic airliner was coming, Patterson even predicted that in time space ships would carry passengers from New York to Manila in two hours. But he stubbornly refused to be stampeded into ordering the French-British Concorde, designed to fly at 1,200-miles-per-hour and promised for delivery in 1970 — or into buying sight-unseen the FAA-inspired 1,800-miles-per-hour SST at a wild guess cost of $25 million per airplane. In 1965, Patterson had a call from the FAA asking why United was the only major airline that hadn't made a deposit — $100,000 per plane — on these visionary airliners of the future.

"We're not ordering now because I like to know what an airplane will cost, when it will be delivered, and how much it will

earn, before I buy it," he explained. "But even if we haven't put up any money, we've invested a lot of work and our Bill Mentzer is chairman of the airline industry SST group. We want to know more about SSTs than any other airline."

By 1966, this "investment in work" had paid off to the point where the United management felt safe in securing delivery positions on SSTs, both French and American.

Patterson also had initial misgivings about the 500 to 1,000-passenger "jumbo jets" designed by both Boeing and Lockheed primarily for military troop movement. Overseas airlines ordered them for passengers, too. He thought they had built-in, people-handling problems not inherent in the 200-passenger DC-8-61s he ordered from Douglas Aircraft early in 1965.

One corollary of the jet age has revealed Patterson's obsession for safety and comfort of passengers. Even before the jetliners complicated the mass moving of people, he was fighting "sardine seating" in commercial airliners. Oddly enough, Patterson was the first airline operator to try coach flights to lure people who had yet to make their first flights off the highways and the rails and into the air. This was in 1939 when United experimented with special coach flights at reduced fares between Los Angeles and San Francisco. It was a test that came to an inconclusive end in 1940 when the military commandeered half United's fleet of DC-3s.

Paradoxically, after the war ended and when the non-skeds

rushed into the air with bargain flights, Patterson fought coach service. When Capital Airlines launched coach flights on the Chicago-New York route and TWA and American met the competition with their own coach service, he held off for a year, on the theory that "coach traffic is first-class business you take away from yourself." But he soon found that rivals' reduced coach fares were luring passengers out of United planes. In 1950 he reluctantly ordered some of the Mainliners modified to coach configuration. Insisting that crowding passengers into maximum high-density seating was a hazard, he limited the seats in United's early DC-4 airplanes to 44. Other airlines crowded in 66 seats. They protested to the CAB that the United configuration was unfair competition. The CAB agreed, and authorized United to increase the DC-4 seating configuration to 54. Rivals still flew with 66 seats. Coach flights took off at odd hours, often at night, when the mail planes were otherwise empty anyway. Passengers could bring their own box lunches or order them from the airline for $2 when they bought tickets. The idea behind "coach" was to pull landlubbers into airliners with bargain fares, then upgrade them to first-class passengers later. It didn't work out that way. The majority of passengers soon were riding coach, leaving many first-class seats unoccupied. But, to their surprise, the airlines found that they were making as much money per square foot of airplane floor space from the crowded coaches as from the more spacious higher-priced first-class seats.

The battle of the classes had an important impact on the jet age. Satisfied that "coach was here to stay," Patterson insisted that United's jetliners, with the exception of the Caravelles, have cabins wide enough for six-abreast coach seating. The jetliners were equipped with movable partitions to separate the first-class passengers up front, where the airplane was supposed to be quieter, from the coach crowd in the back. Month after month, the partitions moved forward as the coach traffic mushroomed and the first-class passengers thinned ranks. When Patterson learned that government agencies and big companies were ordering their people to go coach to save money, he decided that the time had come to do something about the odd turn of events that was depriving United's best customers, the business travelers, of the hospitality of air travel it had taken two decades to develop.

His solution was "one class," a five-abreast configuration for the entire jetliner, and no partition in the cabin. He broached this idea in a talk before travel agents in Las Vegas, pointing out that the air fare schedules had become a nightmare. There were over 20 possible rate combinations between Miami and San Francisco, for example. The cost to the travel agents and to the airlines of calculating these intricate fares ran into the millions. Why not wipe them all out and start at scratch again with a single fare for everybody? His one-class talk got a big play in the newspapers. Patterson received hundreds of letters from both travelers and travel agents urging him to try the plan.

He decided on a test early in 1963 on the Chicago-San Francisco route. Several Boeing 720s about to be delivered were modified to a new seating configuration, two seats on one side of a wide aisle, three on the other. The seats were wider than those in coach sections, and the center seat in the trio was extra wide. One-fare service included a libation on the house, followed by an appetizing meal. Everybody aboard the jetliner enjoyed the same service. The fare was $5.55 above coach and $24.40 below first-class for the flight between San Francisco and Chicago. The one-class test was such a rousing success that Patterson had several DC-8s modified to the new configuration and extended it to transcontinental service. He thought his rivals would switch to one-class, too, to meet United's competition and at the same time unravel the tangle of fares that had grown up Topsy-like over the years.

He guessed right about air travelers but wrong about his rivals. C. R. Smith, militant head of American Airlines, didn't like the one-class innovation and undertook to undermine it by cutting first-class fares to $7.50 above one-class for transcontinental flights. TWA went along with American. Both airlines offered family plan rates, one-half off for wives and children, on coach as well as first-class flights. This effectively sabotaged United's one-class service. Patterson appealed to the CAB, which backed American and

We'd Rather Be Best Than Biggest

SOME OF OUR COMPETITORS *think we absorbed Capital Airlines to make United the biggest airline in the country, which it is. But that isn't why we took over Capital. We don't care particularly about running the largest airline. We would rather run the best airline, whether it's the largest or not. We took over Capital because I could see that if they went into bankruptcy, it would affect the jetliner financing of all airlines. Also, the jobs of 7,000 Capital employees were in jeopardy, as were the investments of 14,000 stockholders. They were the victims of management's mismanagement. Some of our rivals thought that we had bought a corporate corpse, but we worked hard to bring it back to health. We made sure that the former Capital people who joined the United force were not second-class employees in any way. They all got more money and better security and they have become some of United's best assets. We take more pride in that than in being the largest airline. If that had been our goal we could have accomplished it right after the war by continuing to fly to Alaska and Japan, which we had been doing as a war service. But that would have involved a subsidy and we didn't want to be running a subsidized airline. We chose to wait a few years and become the biggest airline without any help from anybody.*

W.A.P.

TWA. Patterson had to do something and fast. The United sales staff came up with a new idea, three classes — Red, White and Blue — on the same jetliner, with two partitions. Red, up front, would be first-class. White, in the middle, would be standard, at one-class fares. Blue, in back, would be a new coach fare, still lower than the old coach. With misgivings, Patterson agreed.

"That's where I made a great mistake," he reflected, later. "I should have lowered the one-class fares and fought it out. It doesn't make much sense to have three kinds of fares and services on the same plane. Some of our competitors refer to the one-class idea as 'Patterson's folly.' It wasn't a folly, nor was it a failure. One-class was sabotaged by competitors, with CAB's blessing.

"If we had hung onto one-class a little longer, all the major airlines might have gone along eventually and the simplified fare structure would be saving millions for both the airlines and the public. My prediction is that when our economy levels off and all airlines are scrambling to reduce costs, one-class will come back. With the millions spent on in-flight movies and on gourmet service for first-class passengers, there is little or no profit in the front section of the jetliners. In the final analysis, it is the customer who pays the bill."

Most of Patterson's battles with competitors and with the CAB over coach service have been on the grounds of safety. What spurred him to action was a visit to Midway Airport one day to see how long it took a coach plane to unload its passengers. After the people had spewed out of the cabin he mounted the steps to see what condition it was in. To his amazement he found two mothers still trying to collect belongings and herd five small children out the narrow aisle.

"If this plane had blown a tire or there were a fire, this would be murder," he thought. When he returned to his office he wired the maintenance base to remove a middle row of seats from all coach planes, thus making the seating five abreast. The CAB, which had approved the high-density seating, promptly ruled that United could not offer coach fares unless the seats were restored. Instead of complying, Patterson took his case to the people in an advertisement entitled, "Which Comes First, Safety or Economics?" published in major newspapers along United's routes. The CAB backed down.

The fight flared with intensity in 1963 when another airline announced a $100 "economy" service between California and Hawaii. To make the low fare possible, they put 187 seats into Boeing 707 jetliners. Patterson protested to the FAA this time, contending that in an emergency 187 passengers would be trapped while the jetliner burned or sank into the ocean. The FAA ordered an evacuation test. When Patterson saw a movie of the evacuation, he exploded:

"That's not a test. Nobody who came out of that plane was over 45. The women were all in slacks. Attendants with ladders were helping them down."

Patterson ordered tests in United jets, in San Francisco and Chicago, with typical passengers in their usual travel attire. To make the test more realistic, neither pilots nor stewardesses were told in advance which exits would be available for evacuation. After the doors were closed, the pilot announced the emergency over the intercom. Smoke bombs were exploded to add to the realism. With FAA and press representatives watching, it took three and one-half minutes to evacuate 174 passengers. In a second test, with a wider aisle, fewer seats and better chutes, 126 passengers got out of the plane in 90 seconds. When evidence of these tests was presented to the CAB, which had approved the other airline's seating, a hearing was postponed and the airline reduced the number of seats on its Hawaii and Puerto Rico flights. United matched the $100 economy fare between California and Hawaii with a 120-seat configuration, which the CAB approved later for all jetliner coach flights, both over water and crosscountry.

"Am I being oversensitive about my moral obligation?" asks Patterson. "I don't think so. I am convinced that air transportation will progress only in proportion to its safety record. Without safety, you do not have a service which is acceptable to the public or to our employees. Safety cannot be discussed in the same breath with economics. Safety must always take precedence."

Even in the struggling days when dollars were scarce, Patterson always somehow found enough of them to pay for safety innovations. In 1948, he found half a million of them to equip United's long-range DC-6 fleet with static-free OMNI range finders that enabled United pilots to fly around the weather instead of following the radio beams through the storm fronts. This investment paid off dramatically the following year when United planes completed 89 percent of their flights during the paralyzing blizzard of 1949 that tied up ground transportation for days. Electronic "seeing eyes" have aroused Patterson's enthusiasm ever since Thorp Hiscock's two-way radio gave pilots constant communication with ground stations. In 1954, he invested $4 million in airborne radar sets for the noses of all United planes. These new electronic eyes enabled pilots to see through clouds and spot hailstorms or the furious, swirling hearts of thunderheads, then fly around them. Another big safety investment came in 1957, when United Mainliners were equipped with ILS radar landing eyes, a revolutionary innovation that eventually reduced "stacking" over cloud-hidden airports. Still another was the use of cloud-seeding to disperse fogs over airports long enough to land airliners in safety.

"Our main job now is to refine and simplify everything we have and everything we do," explained Patterson, just before he turned the airline over to the younger generation. "We can't afford to be half-modern and half-obsolete. We have too many kinds of planes and services and rates. When we get delivery of the 737s, we should be able to reduce our six types of planes to four. It will show up dramatically in the service we give the public and in our economics.

"It always takes some visionaries to get a new show on the road," he added. "They may not be around to give an accounting later, but they are needed to start the acting."

In Patterson's case, he was not only the visionary who innovated revolutionary new airliners; he was on hand to pay the bills.

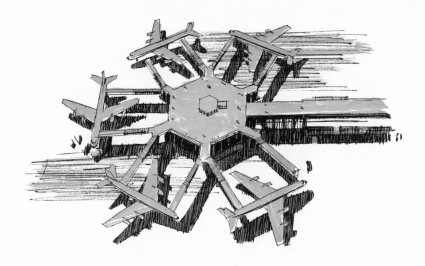

CHAPTER VIII

A Lot of Pat Rubbed Off

Even to United colleagues who have rubbed shoulders with him since before United Air Lines took shape, Patterson's unquenchable thirst for the whole truth about people, planes, and policies has been a source of wonderment. "Pat's always been looking for something," recalls one United vice president. "Anytime, day or night, he's been ready to sit down and explore any idea that might yield whatever he was seeking."

Explained another, "Pat's a perfectionist. He sets high standards and practices them. Sometimes they're so high others have a hard time living up to them. He's always been a do-it-now man. He believes in delegating authority — but he likes to look over shoulders to see that things get done promptly. He's always looking ahead to the next step as the jumping off point for the step after that."

These comments open a window to a complex, agile, and fertile mind. One observation that all of his long-time co-workers stress is that "a lot of Pat rubbed off on us." In few, if any, other companies has the stamp of the builder and shaper so permeated the ranks. This Patterson "rub-off" was understandable when the United family was small enough for him to know every employee personally. The remarkable aspect is that it continued as the payroll exploded from 1,400 people in 1934 when he slipped into the pilot's seat, to 37,000 in 1966 when he turned the wheel over to the younger generation. A lot more of Patterson imprinted itself on the airline industry and on the federal agencies that have come and gone as Congress tested various means of regulating the fabulous young utility that was revolutionizing life in these United States and in other lands as well.

A favorite Patterson epigram has been, "In the airline business a lot of moss grows on an old policy." Another is "Let's remember we're running a 600-mile-an-hour industry." Patterson has made it a practice to take frequent looks at the moss on policies he laid down a decade back — or even a year ago — and to welcome critical looks by his staffers at policies that may be gathering moss.

"If you differ with him sincerely, it's okay," observed one of his long-time associates. "But try and double talk and you're out."

A handy Patterson pattern for winning friends has been to open-mindedly fathom the motives behind the other fellow's point of view, right or wrong. One of his favorite openers in replies to irate letters from passengers is, "I would say that you gave us a well-deserved kick in the pants," after which he can tell his side of the story to a more receptive audience.

During his 32 years as United's generator, Patterson has experimented persistently, searching for the right elastic structure to administer a far-flung airway whose planes could race the sun daily 5,000 miles from New York to Honolulu. The perfect organizational set-up was not easy to find.

"The main difference between one airline and another is personality," he once observed. "How can the president get this idea across to the people who are the airline's personality in a hundred communities? For one thing, by not feeling too important. The heads of most big companies become myths. In my scheme,

A Salute to the Stewardesses

Wᴇ ʜᴀᴅ ᴀ ʟᴜᴄᴋʏ ʙʀᴇᴀᴋ, *in our service to the public, back in 1930. We had decided to hire some men as couriers for our planes, when an imaginative young nurse from San Francisco's French Hospital named Ellen Church came in and told our manager, "You should have nurses as attendants on the planes." So we made the switch to stewardesses and the result has given air transport everywhere an atmosphere different from that of all other forms of transportation. This was a great turning point in our business. To me, Ellen Church walking into our San Francisco office at the crucial moment was like the accidental discovery of penicillin. Had we hired men couriers as we planned, some of them would still be with us, wearing shiny blue serge suits. Instead, we have had young women bubbling with the romance of flying, a refreshing and relaxing feature of air travel. It was our good fortune that we got started off with a unique atmosphere from which we could build a personal, conscientious, and satisfying service which has spread to all of the world's major airlines. Ellen Church was the Florence Nightingale of air transport. She created a fine, adventurous new profession for thousands of young women.*

W.A.P.

the president is just the opposite; he's out there with the people, as a living personality."

One of Patterson's long-time hunts has been for a flexible company configuration, adjustable to the changing speeds of air-liners. Over the years he has been torn between divisional and centralized operation. In 1934 he began with a stretched out divi-sional system in which each of the original parts functioned almost as independent airlines, with Chicago-based, new-born United Air Lines Transport Corporation as the web that held them together. This loose arrangement had so many disadvantages that he had to pull the network into a single centralized system while he sought a better way of delegating responsibility. His next inspiration was two geographic divisions, one for operations east of Chicago, the other the merged western lines. Each division had a general man-ager and staff. The advent of faster planes soon made this scheme obsolete, and Patterson switched again to centralized management. But he still sought the perfect divisional system.

"That's a mistake on which I had to be burned three times," he admits, wryly.

His last burn was when he undertook to divide up United Air Lines by departments. This divisional split-up coincided with a temporary love affair between Pat Patterson and the mile-high city of Denver, Colorado. The United family had grown to 13,000, and Patterson felt that too many of them were concentrated in Chicago. He had an idea that "our operating people can do a better job of running the airline in an atmosphere of seclusion from finance and policy." A firm of consultants had surveyed cities served by United Air Lines and had spotlighted Denver as the community with the best living conditions of any United center. It happened to be the exact geographic hub of the United network after Honolulu became an airport of call.

The Denver city fathers underwrote a sizable bond issue in 1947 to build a handsome two-story building on the edge of Staple-ton Airfield, which United could lease as headquarters for Flight Operations, with 3,000 people, and Transportation Services, with 8,000 more. These employees were scattered over the airline, of course, but they would look to Denver, rather than Chicago, as the headquarters of the executive staffs of the two departments which did the actual operating of the airline. While "the great exodus to Denver" was in motion, Patterson decided to concentrate Engineering and Maintenance in a huge new base at San Francisco International Airport known, in United vernacular, as SFOMB. Headquarters for Vice President Jack A. Herlihy, San Francisco became United's largest concentration of employees. Patterson kept the Sales, Finance and Property, Economic Planning, Public Relations, Law, and Medical departments under his wing in the United executive building across the street from Chicago's Midway Airport.

This unique division-by-departments began to gather moss almost immediately. Too many top executives were scattered over the airline when they were needed for huddles in Chicago. Patterson was soon complaining that "whenever anything goes wrong we have to conduct a witch hunt to find the fellow who is responsible." United staffers began to refer to the Denver GHQ as "the United country club." Denver's city fathers began tapping airport earnings for general municipal funds and Patterson had to take them to task in a talk before the Denver Chamber of Commerce, warning that they might be driving a $16 million annual payroll out of town.

Even SFOMB, the $14 million San Francisco maintenance base, was referred to as "United's folly," a rank misnomer. "I'll tell you how much of a folly it is," Patterson explained to a group of bankers. "It has reduced manhours for overhaul of aircraft so much that we are paying for the base with six years' savings. I call that a good investment."

SFOMB continued to expand and save dollars for United, becoming the model for maintenance bases of a number of airlines, domestic and foreign. But Patterson couldn't pinpoint similar savings in the move of Operations and Transportation Services to Denver. Along about 1960, he concluded that he had been burned enough by the divisional will o' the wisp. He reversed his thinking to the "one roof" concept — all of United's top management under one big top, except for Engineering and Maintenance in San Francisco. Flight training remained in Denver. His one roof was a shining, functional $7 million structure newly risen out of the Illinois countryside in Elk Grove township nine miles northwest of Chicago's sprawling O'Hare International Airport.

The spacious headquarters, three floors including basement, represented Patterson's new image of a model jet age airline GHQ. It was far enough from O'Hare to have quiet, but near enough to the world's busiest airport to catch planes to anywhere. By jetliner, no United station, not even Honolulu, was more than eight hours from the executive offices. Rising out of a 51-acre farm, this new office complex was a complete corporate community. It had 11 acres of stretchable offices, an airline academy for training everybody but the flight crews, communications nerve centers, a medical clinic, dining facilities — surrounded by 40 acres of lawns, trees, a lake and parking areas. When the trek back from Denver and the move to the country from Midway was completed during the winter of 1961-62, with 3,200 United people under one roof, Patterson felt that his three-decade search for the right milieu for running an airline had been rewarded. The one-roof move was little short of providential; it was the jumping off point for the next big jump, namely, the sudden absorption of Capital Airlines into the United system that same year.

The merger highlighted some key facets in the Patterson philosophy of doing business. Taking over Capital rates as one of

Patterson's more daring decisions. Capital had fallen on such hard times that it was "a corporate corpse that didn't know it was dead," as he put it. Most of United's rivals, soaring like buzzards waiting to pick on the bones when Capital finally succumbed, insist that Patterson took the big gamble to make United the country's biggest airline. They misread the Patterson mind. Welding Capital, the nation's sixth largest airline, onto United, the second largest, did create the Number 1 airline in size, but this was not his primary motive in taking the long chance.

Patterson has always been jealously proud of the airline industry's record of solvency. He likes to point out that no important airline ever has had to go through the bankruptcy wringer that squeezed out the investments of thousands of shareholders in railroads. His thinking is that of an airline statesman who devoutly believes that failure of one airline is a black eye for the entire industry. He has backed this belief with hard cash. In 1947, he dug into United's reserves to lend $1 million to Terrell C. Drinkwater, newly appointed president of Western Air Lines, to keep Western afloat until Patterson could take over a Western commitment at Douglas Aircraft for five new DC-6s and pay Western $2,750,000 for its Denver-Los Angeles route. The transfusion enabled Western to rebound to vigorous health and become one of United's toughest competitors in the west. More important in Patterson's thinking, this purchase, with the CAB's blessing, established an important principle, namely, that an airline's routes were more than mere licenses to fly between two points; they were its assets and its property, like a railroad's rails.

This was a key factor in the Capital debacle. Five other airlines wanted to divide up Capital's routes, picking up those that looked profitable. No other airline was willing to take over Capital as a whole, the bad routes with the good.

Patterson had been burned twice already on proposed mergers with Capital or its predecessor, Pennsylvania-Central Airlines. In 1938, when he had agreed to take over hard-pressed Pennsylvania, its bankers blocked the deal. In 1955, when Capital's dashing president, former pilot J. H. "Slim" Carmichael, proposed merger of his hungry airline with United, Patterson suggested that the two companies' boards get together for merger talks.

"Let's let them decide who will be president if we merge," said Patterson.

By the time the joint directors' meeting took place in New York, Capital was flying its new Viscount turbo-prop airliners, just delivered by Vickers-Armstrong of England. First prop-jets to fly in this country, the Viscounts were pulling passengers off United, TWA, and American DC-7s on the busy New York-Chicago run. The outlook was so rosy that Carmichael no longer wished to merge.

Five years later, the picture was dark. Carmichael was out. Capital still owed $34 million on its fleet of 68 Viscounts. The 375-mile-per-hour turbo-props were no match for rival 575-mile-per-hour straight jets. Capital had no credit to buy jetliners. The airline's traffic on its longer routes had almost evaporated. Vickers-Armstrong had filed suit to recover some of the millions still owed on the Viscounts. In desperation, the Capital board drafted a former director of the company, Thomas D. Neelands, Jr., New York financier and merger expert, to try to save the ailing airline by consolidation into a strong, thriving company. Neelands agreed to try to work the miracle — without compensation. He sought out Patterson and laid the cards face up on the table. United was the only airline vigorous enough to breathe life back into the corporate corpse.

Patterson's first response was "No." He had had his two burns with proposed Capital mergers. Then he began to brood over the consequences of his "No." A major bankruptcy in the airline industry was unthinkable. It would be a financial catastrophe just at a time when the country's airline operators were asking the investing public for $2 billion to pay for fleets of jetliners. He thought about the plight of 7,000 Capital employees, whom he termed "victims of management's mismanagement." And the 14,000 shareholders would be washed out; many of them were actual or potential buyers of stock in United and other airlines. The British plane builders were holding the sack for millions. Finally, there were Capital's routes, which the CAB had extended with open hands between major population centers of the eastern third of the country in a futile effort to provide Capital with more traffic. These routes had merely worsened the competition for Capital. But joined to the United network, they could fan out the system into an eastern traffic pattern comparable to that on the Pacific Coast. After much cogitation, Patterson reversed his "No" to a "Yes"—with provisos.

The conditions were that the merger talks had to be strictly on the quiet; United would do no bidding against rivals; if the CAB lopped off any of Capital's routes, the deal was off. Neelands readily agreed. Patterson called in Curtis Barkes, senior vice president for finance, and asked him to fly to New York to carry on negotiations with Neelands and the Vickers-Armstrong representatives. Then Patterson caught a plane for Seattle to throw the financial sleuths off the scent. But he admits that during the month of negotiations he looked over Curtis Barkes' shoulder by telephone several times a day.

On July 28, 1960, he turned up in Washington, D.C., for a joint press conference with Neelands to announce that the merger agreement had been signed. They went over to CAB headquarters to explain their merger plan. Patterson had some conditions to lay down there, too. One, if any Capital routes were tossed to hungry rivals, the deal was off. The other was, the CAB must approve the merger in six months, or all bets were off. Equally eager to forestall a bankruptcy, the CAB held hearings with unprecedented speed and, despite objections from five airlines and seven unions, okayed the merger. Capital came into the United fold on June 1, 1961, and ceased to exist as a separate entity.

Later, commenting upon the CAB's unusual action, Alan S. Boyd, the agency's chairman at the time, said, "I'm convinced today, as I was at the time, that Pat undertook that merger for the benefit of the air transportation industry. And there were some very real doubts at that time that the merger was going to be an asset to United Air Lines."

Patterson had dark moments when he had doubts, too. Absorbing Capital was such a huge bite that it gave the entire

United system an acute case of traffic gollywobbles. Flight Operations had to steal jetliners from nearly every run to soup up service and regain passengers on the former Capital routes. Hundreds of employees had to be transferred to new stations. To help them finance purchases of new homes, Patterson agreed to buy their old homes at market prices. At one time, United was involved in the purchase of homes approaching a value of $15 million which were eventually sold at a loss well in excess of $1 million. It was part of the price of merger.

"For the first few months, I thought the world had caved in on us," Patterson recalled later. "On one bad day I had 52 letters complaining about United service. I told my secretary to write all these people and send their money back. Only three kept it."

Steadily, order emerged from the chaos. The United-Capital merger planning committee — six junior executives from each airline, headed by United's Warren Alberts — set up by Patterson as soon as the merger papers were signed, had done an outstanding job of meshing into one team the two divergent phalanxes of workers described as "a very hungry group of people married to a group that was well fed." This was Marvin Whitlock, Capital's senior vice president for operations and maintenance, speaking. Whitlock, who quickly advanced to senior vice president for operations with United, added:

"Capital was a get-along-without airline. United was one that bought only the best. It worked out well for the Capital people. The United family went more than half-way to welcome them. Anyone willing to try found a happy home."

One reason the people-merger worked so smoothly was that Patterson decreed at the outset that there would be no second-class employees working for United. Since Capital's pay scale was lower than United's, every former Capital employee got a raise with his first pay check, as well as training for better positions, medical care, retirement and other fringe benefits — even to baby blankets for the newborn. At the time of the merger, Capital had 6,000 labor grievances, more than all the other airlines in the country together. After the merger, all but a handful evaporated.

Why We Are Regulated

Aᴌᴛʜᴏᴜɢʜ ɪ ᴀᴍ *associated with an industry that's been government-regulated for many years, I wear no shackles. Our company and the other trunklines are self-sufficient. We don't receive a dime of government subsidy. We're subject to the same economic forces that affect business in general. We have some requirements far more demanding than in other types of business. One of the pitfalls to be sidestepped in a regulated industry is the tendency to blame our troubles on the government. Grousing about the loss of liberty will not cause restrictive government agencies to go away. They're here and here to stay. And unless the facts behind their origin are understood, there may be more. I've seen many of the executive agencies come into being— the SEC, the NLRB, the FTC, the CAB, the FAA, and others. Once they're born, they thrive and grow. I've concluded that the moral to be drawn from their existence is this: when you abuse liberty, you lose liberty. Trace the events that led to the origin of the restrictive agencies and you'll invariably find that a few men, or a group of men, chose to interpret liberty as the right to do as they pleased without regard to ethics or to the interests of others. Their operations antagonized the public and Congress took action. It's as simple as that.*

W.A.P.

Merging the traffic patterns of the two systems was another story. Vickers-Armstrong took back 18 Viscounts. The 50 that now flew the United shield replaced obsolete DC-4s and DC-3s on shorter runs. They began to make money. As fast as Caravelles and 720s became available, flight time on longer Capital runs was cut to jet speed. United's longer-range jetliners made such good time on transcontinental flights that they could add a north-south flight to the day's work. Traffic boomed on the former Capital routes twice as fast as on regular United routes. By the end of 1962, Patterson knew that the transfusion had worked. The "corpse" had come to life and was earning good returns for United. The big gamble had paid off, not only for United Air Lines but for the entire airline industry.

"We took over Capital at the right time," explained Patterson just before he retired. "Some of our rivals thought we'd bought a liability. We bought at 50 cents on the dollar, through an exchange of stock, but within five years United shares had advanced so much in value that everyone got $2 on the dollar."

The CAB's prompt action to his blunt terms for the United-Capital merger pointed up another significant side of the Patterson impact on people. Ever since the "airmail purge" that indirectly made him president of United Air Lines in 1934, Patterson has been the forthright, sometimes undiplomatic spokesman for the airline industry in Washington, D.C. Scarcely a year had passed without a call for him to testify before congressional committees or at hearings of the ever-changing boards that have laid down safety rules, regulated fares, granted routes, or bolstered weak airlines with subsidies. He has never minced words in his opinions and has always suspected that he was in the Washington doghouse.

In 1947, for example, following a series of airliner crashes, he needled a Senate sub-committee for $200 million to enable the then anemic CAA to equip 200 of the country's airports with high intensity lights, improved radar landing controls, and fog dispersal devices. The next year he was blasting the CAB for vacillating, do-nothing policies, and hampering regulations. In 1949, he told a Senate Commerce sub-committee, "No one in the CAB or its

148

staff has ever crossed the threshold of United's doors to see for himself the methods we are employing."

Instead of winning him a permanent berth in the Washington doghouse, the unvarnished truth won him a respected status as the Number 1 airline industry statesman. As Alan S. Boyd put it, when Undersecretary of Commerce for Transportation, "He has been a conservative, candid, competent and cheerful individual, exemplary of the best qualities of the people in the air transportation industry. Most important, in my mind, Pat Patterson has been aware of the dynamism of the industry and has been willing to do something about it — to undertake new risks in times when there were more doubters than believers."

The United-Capital union, coincident with the switchover to jetliners, added up to a veritable revolution for the airline. The orderly upheaval of the early sixties moved the United center of gravity eastward. The north-south routes inherited from Capital more than balanced the pioneer Pacific routes. The jetliners shrank United's geography time-wise to one half what it was in the fifties. The price tag on the jetliner fleet which Patterson and his planners projected to provide jet service on all United routes was around $2 billion — more than all the resources of the Wells Fargo Bank when Patterson made that first risky loan to those flying machine men.

To pay United's way into the jet age, Patterson had to tap vast new reserves of capital — $160 million from three insurance companies, $165 million from 30 banks in cities along the airline, still larger sums from shareholders. But the jetliners earned money faster and paid for themselves and expensive new installations on the ground far more speedily than anyone dreamed they would. The jet era launched United into more fantastic high finance than Patterson could have imagined when he took over as head of the airline. By 1965, he was chief of an airways empire with assets just under $1 billion and yearly revenues topping $750 million. All this had grown during his three decades as United's head out of a nest egg of $4 million in the bank and a fleet of 60 Boeing 247s worth even less than the airline's cash.

By his sixtieth birthday, October 1, 1959, Patterson was diligently hunting the man to manage this airways empire when he retired at 65. There was no shortage of talent in his top echelon. Any one of several executives could have taken the helm in an emergency. His "promote from within" policy had yielded a top-flight crop of vice presidents. His right-hand man in finance, Curtis Barkes, he had discovered "in the broom closet," as he put it, after Barkes had spent two decades since joining NAT at routine accounting tasks while treasurers came and departed. Barkes was named vice president-finance and property in 1949 and executive vice president in 1961. This move paid off handsomely when Barkes handled the borrowing of millions for jetliners and when he negotiated the terms of the Capital merger.

Senior vice president Robert E. Johnson, who had come to Chicago with Patterson from Seattle in 1931 to handle public relations, had emerged as United's marketing expert. "Bob always knew what I was thinking without even asking me," Patterson has said, with appreciation. Another senior vice president whose radar blipped the Patterson mind instinctively was Russ Ahrens. In the Cheyenne shops, Patterson found a young MIT graduate, W. C. Mentzer, who succeeded another MIT engineer, former airmail pilot Jack Herlihy, as senior vice president for engineering and maintenance. On the legal staff, he spotted another potential executive vice president, Charles F. McErlean. These and several other veteran United executives were invited by Patterson to a dinner one evening in 1958 at Chicago's University Club.

It turned out to be a dinner with a typically Patterson flair. Ostensibly, the occasion was a welcome for several newly appointed vice presidents to the United executive dining room. But everybody present sensed that something more important was in the wind. It was. After a lively dinner, the genial host made a short talk which ended with the announcement that the next president of United Air Lines would have to be at least fifteen years younger than William Allan Patterson. The board of directors had so decreed, at Patterson's instigation, so that the next president would have to live with his decisions, for better or for worse. There was a

Public Relations Is a Way of Life

Sᴛʀɪᴘᴘᴇᴅ ᴏꜰ ᴀʟʟ *the cloudy thinking that surrounds the term, what is "good public relations"? Well, let's answer with another question. What is good private relations? It is mutual understanding, respect, and sometimes affection. It is the warm handclasp, the ready and sincere smile. It is the genuine concern, the solicitous inquiry, the unsolicited help, the spontaneous tribute. It is a high and continuing regard for the other fellow. Multiply the friendly relations you have with one person by a million, substitute in place of yourself and a friend an institution and the general public, and you have public relations.*

I also think that public relations is the evaluation by the public of your particular philosophy of doing business. You must first have a philosophy of business before you can transmit it to others. If your philosophy is good, you make a sound and favorable impression; if your philosophy is wrong, there is no sound basis for a good public relations program. I don't think a public relations man can pull a rabbit out of the hat. Public relations is a message that you transmit to the public by the manner in which you do business.

W.A.P.

silence as everyone looked around the table to mentally check the ages of those present, followed by a spontaneous laugh. At one swoop Patterson had eliminated everybody in United's top bracket of executives as presidential timber.

The hurdle behind him, Patterson launched an on-the-quiet manhunt among the airline's younger executives for a future president. A score of bright young men were quietly shifted to new duties to test their potentials. The hunt narrowed down to four and then, by 1962, to one. Out at the San Francisco maintenance base, Jack Herlihy had a young industrial engineer, George E. Keck, a graduate of the great depression's CCC camps who had worked his way through the University of Illinois. Keck joined United fresh out of the Army following the war, worked first in Chicago, then at the San Francisco maintenance base. There he caught Jack Herlihy's eye. "That fellow can handle any job on the airline," Herlihy reported to Patterson. Keck had a chance to demonstrate his potentials in a newly created post, executive vice president and general manager for the entire United system. In September, 1963, when Patterson moved up to the newly created position of chairman of the board, George E. Keck became United's second youthful president. Patterson was still chief executive officer, with power of final decision, but Keck was operating the world's biggest airliner fleet.

The Scottish caution in Patterson asserted itself at this point. He decided upon a new management chart that would enable him gradually to shift duties to Keck, but still permit an occasional Patterson look over everybody's shoulder. Altogether, this meant some 32,000 shoulders, United's payroll after the merger. Patterson kept 2,000 of these shoulders in his own area, as chairman of the board. These included the vice presidents for finance and property, for community relations, and the legal and medical departments. The other 30,000 he turned over to Keck to be divided about equally between the vice presidents for operations and for marketing.

This reshuffle came at a propitious time, just as United entered a period of almost fabulous growth. Traffic, both passenger and cargo, boomed. Each year of the mid-sixties showed an increase of

18 to 30 percent over the one before. The jetliners paid for themselves and kept on earning without wearing out. For the first time, Patterson could feel that he had airplanes that were not outmoded by time of delivery. The visionary supersonics were a decade off. United shares zoomed up on the stock market, were split by the directors, then soared anew. By 1965, United's jetliners were carrying more passengers than those of all foreign airlines together. The Hundred Thousand Mile Club, an inspiration of the forties to honor steady air travelers and to provide a handy forum for Patterson ideas about safety, fares, or service, had almost 250,000 members, who happily hung United shields on their office walls. Any way anybody looked at United, the airline looked good.

Instead of bringing him joy, the rosy outlook plummeted Pat Patterson into a wrenching soul struggle. With United thriving and a strong young president at the helm, was there any sound reason why he should stay on as chairman and chief executive officer beyond the official company retirement age of 65? The board of directors wanted him to continue until he was 70, by special dispensation. His health was good. He was director of several other outstanding companies, but United was his life. His hobbies were his grandchildren, golf, and people. Could they keep him as occupied and happy as his powerful desk at the executive offices and his official trips over the United system on the jetliners?

To reach this, his hardest decision, he retired to his desert retreat at Borrego Springs, California, where fellow members of the De Anza country club handed him the president's flag to run up above his modest home overlooking the golf course. Probably only two people, Vera Patterson and Dr. George Kidera, realized what a battle Patterson was fighting with himself by day and by night that mid-winter. "He always needs ten days to stew out a big decision," explained Kidera. "This time he needed more time." When Patterson returned to Chicago, he was ready with his hard decision — not to be a candidate for re-election as United's chairman of the board at the annual stockholders' meeting in April, 1966.

He was stepping out, he explained, so that "those who are charged with responsibility for the future will be free to use their own initiative and wisdom in the policies they establish. They should have no inhibitions concerning the past." Even more of a shocker was his unequivocal decision to withdraw his name as a candidate for the United board of directors.

"My continued presence on the board would create inhibitions," he said.

He was looking over no more shoulders. With typical Patterson candor, he admitted: "I've spent too much of my life with and for United Air Lines not to be reluctant to cut it off. But I know you can't be a part-time leader. You can't make good decisions unless you are involved — or at least informed — on a day-to-day basis."

In 1958, on their own initiative, United's directors had voted to give Patterson a ten-year contract as consultant, to start whenever he retired. A consultant didn't have to look over shoulders, or make decisions.

"What makes this transition easy is that I am in perfect accord with the Patterson philosophy," said Keck. "His personal philosophy pervades this whole organization. It stands out among management and the people on the line. Pat has had a true and sincere belief that he had an obligation to people, whether customers or employees or stockholders. There is a universal respect for United Air Lines on a world-wide basis. This is a great heritage to have. It stems from Pat; he created it. I'm going to carry on his philosophy and principles. I don't know any other."

During his last day as chief executive, April 28, 1966, Patterson presided at the morning meeting of stockholders. It was a standing-room-only gathering, with an air of expectancy. The stockholders, many of them employees, were not interested in dollars and cents; they were on hand to pay tribute to the man who had been "Mr. United" for more than three decades. The opportunity came when publisher Gardner "Mike" Cowles, a United director since 1944, took the gavel out of Patterson's hand and offered this resolution:

"Few persons are granted the opportunity to participate in the shaping of an industry which is to affect profoundly the way of life of millions of people. Even fewer seize the opportunity when presented.

"It was a wise and provident fate which 40 years ago directed the steps of Vern C. Gorst, a pioneer commercial airline operator, to the desk of young William A. "Pat" Patterson in the Wells Fargo Bank of San Francisco. The vision and courage which in the ensuing years have marked Pat's every action were perhaps never more in demand than when he approved a $5,000 loan to a United predecessor 40 years ago, a far more venturesome undertaking than his many multi-million-dollar decisions in recent years.

"Since that time, the eyes of Pat Patterson have been upon the stars, while his feet remained firmly planted on the ground. Always alert to the interests of his shareholders, he early recognized that those interests could not be disassociated from the interests of the public which United served or of the employees who were its blood and bone. First and foremost in his thinking has been the safety of the passengers, regardless of cost or effect on airline earnings. A strong second has been the welfare of United's employees from whom no complaint has ever been too trivial to merit his attention.

"Nothing the shareholders of United can do or say will add to the stature of the man who now steps down as chief executive of the world's greatest airline, but they cannot let this occasion pass without some expression of their great affection and esteem for him.

"NOW, THEREFORE, BE IT RESOLVED that the shareholders of United Air Lines voice their pride in the company which Pat Patterson has created, their appreciation of the leadership which he has provided for a period of more than 30 years, and their hope that, relieved of the burden of executive responsibility, he may find that, for him, the best is yet to come."

The United directors had planned to wind up the retiring chief executive's career with a last luncheon, but Patterson crossed them up.

"I already have a date with some girls," he said, slyly.

The girls were eight of his favorite distaff workers and his daughter, Patty. They had ransacked the lost and found department for appropriate retirement gifts for the boss — an umbrella, a cane, a compass, a fan, a fly swatter "to keep him busy." The serious gifts were a "Boss Number 1" award and a scroll done in verse entitled, "Aloha, Boss." With the gifts and awards under his arm, Patterson hustled off to catch a jetliner to his desert home at Borrego Springs, California.

It was the end of an era for United Air Lines.

Epilogue

It was Pat Patterson's idea that after his last stockholders' meeting and the lively distaff farewell luncheon he could catch a jetliner for his California desert home and slip quietly out of the airline picture. It didn't work out that way. "Without portfolio," as he described his new status, he suddenly became the country's busiest retired president. With wise foresight, the directors kept his chairman of the board office intact, as his consultant's office whenever he wanted to use it. He was still a director of Goodyear Tire & Rubber Company, Westinghouse Electric Corporation, the Harris Trust & Savings Bank (Chicago), Bell & Howell Company, Insurance Company of North America, Gulf & Western Industries, Inc., but at his request not United Air Lines; a trustee of Northwestern University and of Passavant Memorial Hospital in Chicago; an active director in the Chicago Boys' Club and in Junior Achievement, Inc.; and an advisory board member in a dozen civic organizations. An avalanche of letters from well-wishers inundated him. With characteristic Patterson sense of duty he insisted on dictating personal replies until the last letter was answered and signed by his own hand.

Many of the major cities on the United network made plans for a civic luncheon or dinner to honor him. The bounds of stamina forced him to limit these proposed affairs to half a dozen. A great "this is your life" party was sponsored by the Chicago Association of Commerce and Industry, at which the city's mayor presented him with an award for his role in making Chicago the country's busiest air transport mecca, and an annual 'W. A. Patterson Aviation Prize' was established in his honor by the Association. A gathering in Oakland was organized by the East Bay Chamber of Commerce and the Port Commission, at which he was handed a scroll of appreciation from the State of California. At an Atlanta luncheon, the International Council of Industrial Editors named him "Communicator of the Year," a tribute to his effective and steadfast practice of maintaining frank and open communication with employees. In New York, the Aviation Writers Association presented him with the Monsanto Aviation Safety Award for his "most significant and lasting contribution to aviation safety." He was among the first to be named an Honorary Member of the Aerospace Medical Association and at a convention in Las Vegas, the Airline Medical Directors Association bestowed upon him the Aero Medical Award for pioneering United's outstanding medical department, the first time a non-medical man had received the honor. As guest of honor at the Annual Flight Safety Foundation meeting in Madrid, Spain, he received the Flight Safety Foundation-Distinguished Service Award sponsored by Aviation Week and Space Technology Association for his outstanding contributions to air transportation safety. The Clipped Wings, United's alumni stewardesses, at their 25th anniversary voted him honorary membership as godfather of the thriving and high-flying women's profession. In San Francisco, where Patterson sentimentally scheduled the final civic luncheon, a thousand leading citizens gathered to cheer the local boy who did "stick by those flying machine men," following his first doubtful Wells Fargo loan to them, and helped them build the world's largest and strongest airline. Later however, he was given a surprise honor by the Honolulu Chamber of Commerce at a luncheon honoring the home-town boy from the plantation town of Waipahu, Hawaii.

Most gratifying of all to "Mr. United" was the handsome plaque presented by President George Keck on behalf of 38,000 members of the United family at the annual awards dinner in Chicago, bearing the engraved words, "To William Allan Patterson, who gave substance to the Vision in Locksley Hall. Gratefully presented by employees of United Air Lines, whom he led with wisdom, courage and understanding." His former colleagues on the board of directors voted to erect as a part of the executive office complex a William A. Patterson Museum of Air Transportation in which to house models of airliners that grew with United Air Lines, dramatic photographs, and documents, and other historic items marking the milestones in the saga of air transport, all within the business lifespan of Pioneer Patterson. Anybody who wants advice from Consultant Patterson will know where to find him. "But he'll have to come and get it," adds Mr. United. "I'm not looking over anyone's shoulder any more. I am realistic about the status of a consultant. It is only a normal and human characteristic for a new generation of management to have the desire and ambition to make their own niche in the business world, independent of the experience of their predecessors."

Index